COCO CHANEL

Isabelle Fiemeyer

COCO CHANEL
An Essence of Mystery

Translated from the French *Coco Chanel, un parfum de mystère*
by Corey Friedman

First published in the United Kingdom in 2023 by
Thames & Hudson Ltd, 181A High Holborn, London WC1V 7QX

First published in France under the title: *Coco Chanel, un parfum
de mystère* © 1999 Editions Payot & Rivages, Paris; revised and
enlarged edition © 2022 Éditions Payot & Rivages, Paris
This edition © 2023 Thames & Hudson Ltd, London

British Library Cataloguing-in-Publication Data
A catalogue record for this book is available from the
British Library

ISBN 978-0-500-02731-8

Printed and bound in the UK by CPI (UK) Ltd

MIX
Paper | Supporting
responsible forestry
FSC
www.fsc.org   FSC® C171272

Contents

Sometimes with the Heart

Seldom with the Soul

Scarcer once with the Might

Few – love at all.

Emily Dickinson

1
THE RAG DOLL

Courpière, France, 1892. There she is, a child clawing away at brown dirt with her bare hands. Behind her, crosses erected atop a too-low wall thinly veil the gold slopes of the Forez Mountains. Further left, the October hues of Chignore melt into the colours of the sky. Entranced by her task, she is entirely uninterested in the landscape, which she could, for what it's worth, describe down to the very last detail with her eyes closed, so often has she made the steep climb up to this small cemetery that is her kingdom.

She continues to dig, a slim silhouette crouching between the tombstones. Then, slowly and seriously, she begins to bury, one by one, her most cherished treasures collected over the last few months. A pencil case, a white handkerchief, a wooden spoon, all brought home by her father. 'See? I never forget my little Coco,' he says, using the affectionate nickname he gave her at birth. 'Coco,' or 'my little Coco,' he repeats each time he hands her a gift, as if to console her after his long absences. She believes him, overjoyed to feel loved.[1]

A month has passed since she watched him leave, his cart loaded with overalls and underwear, with nightgowns and undershirts – plain, embroidered, pleated, or laced – with corsets, camisoles, and hats. For a month now, she has imagined him criss-crossing the Auvergne region, from market to market. When will he be back? Upon waking, and occasionally at bedtime, she poses the question to her confidant, Julia-Berthe, who is not only her sister but nearly her twin, just one year senior. But it is not until she has stopped waiting for him that her father, preceded often by the sound of a horse-drawn carriage, finally arrives. Coco is always the first to welcome him, the first to throw herself into Albert Chanel's arms the moment his broad body appears in the doorway. It is in an attempt to freeze these memories, to immortalize them, that she buries her father's gifts in a strange ritual. 'This way, everything is truly mine,' she explains to Julia-Berthe.

Crouched in front of a small mound of dirt, stock still despite her numb legs, she remains on the lookout, incapable of giving in, even for an instant, to the silence. Under a dark mass of hair, her two dark eyes peer out. Suddenly, she hears a creak. She expects to see a visitor appear, carrying a pitcher of water. But nothing happens. 'It must have been an animal, or a shifting branch, or even grinding teeth,' she tells herself.

Coco revels in tales of ghosts, of tortured souls who come back to the places where they died. She firmly believes that witches hold their sabbath at a crossroads in the light of dawn. At times, she thinks she can see them on the horizon, bending over immense cauldrons – open wells thought to have run dry – that descend straight to the bowels of the earth. Chasing after her father along the stone paths, she has, on more than one occasion, sighted these huge blisters in the shape of cones or domes. This land, this very personal geography, is one to which she will always lay claim: 'I am the only volcano in Auvergne which has not gone extinct.'

She loves speaking to the dead, 'her dead', as she calls them. She has favourite tombstones. There is the one that leans against the back wall, where a sculpted angel holding a crown in both hands seems to have been half-erased by brutal winds. Another bears a sad inscription that reads 'Died 1878, aged three and a half months'. Coco prays for the stone angel and the faceless child who died too soon. But on Sundays after Mass, she is reluctant – so great is the pain – to go with her mother to the grave of her youngest brother, Augustin, named after her maternal uncle; the boy was delicate from birth and passed away at six months of age. They sometimes go together in a procession, with Alphonse, her younger brother by two years, at the head, followed by Julia-Berthe and the two youngest, Antoinette and Lucien. The eldest, Adrien, a boy who died as a baby, is never spoken of.[2]

Later in life, she will say that she felt protected when alone in her cemetery with her buried objects and 'her' dead strangers. She will call this 'a world of her own, a dream world where she could escape her home's tragic and heavy atmosphere.'[3] Her solitude is not a withdrawal into the shadows: it is a means of survival. Her imagination will fuel her future work, even though she does not know it yet.

If she stretches uncomfortably, she can glimpse some stones arranged in the shape of a cross shining in the distance. That is where she buried her rag doll. Julia-Berthe, the one person who knows about this, is charged with looking after her younger sister but follows Coco only as far as the cemetery before promptly turning around to go home.

'Try to see what she's up to!' orders their mother, who, while concerned about the many missing objects, never has the energy to ask her eldest daughter what she has seen when she returns. Jeanne, with her bewildered eyes and hollow cheeks, is prematurely aged. Usually so brave and hardworking, she now lies bedridden until dusk, lips forming a tired and sad smile whenever one of her children comes near the bed. 'Don't make a sound,' Julia-Berthe says again and again.

Jeanne suffered from a bad chest and her already fragile health was weakened by pregnancies and difficult births, household chores, sewing, and mending. For hours on end, she worked until her eyes were worn out, her back stooped and aching. Most of all, she struggled to follow her husband as he travelled the roads of Puy-de-Dôme and beyond, by cart or by train, from market to market, from fair to fair. She travelled, sometimes pregnant, sometimes coughing and choking, and usually without the children, who remained at home with family. She was consumed by love, madly besotted with her too-handsome husband, and was hurt by his absences and by the affairs she either heard about or imagined.

However, after the birth of Coco in 1883, she began to feel more hopeful. Albert Chanel finally asked her to marry him, even though she had given up on the idea. In truth, it was the family in Courpière who had somewhat forced the marriage proposal, as, after three births, there was an urgent need to make the union official,[4] and thus grant legal recognition to Coco and Julia-Berthe, who had been born out of wedlock.[5] Besides her personal belongings and furniture, the bride-to-be came with 'a sum of five thousand francs in the form of cash or credit',[6] a respectable amount that Albert Chanel nevertheless promptly spent.

She believed that this new status would change everything, that a fickle man could become a faithful spouse. To believe this was not to know Albert, with his dark grey gaze and olive complexion, his brown beard and brown hair, tall for the time at five feet eight inches, an unrepentant seducer that teenage girls blushed at, and women were always drawn to, despite themselves.

Little Coco was proud of her charming father. She told herself there was no way he could be just a salesman, even though he had the patter of one, setting off on the road to sell his meagre goods: 'Albert Chanel, dealer in hosiery and linens of all kinds.'[7] She preferred to picture him as a wine merchant, an explorer, or an adventurer, set out to conquer Auvergne and the rest of the world. Maybe even America, the land where everything was possible, whose name she had heard people say with a mixture of fear and wonder: 'Gone to America'. Many years later, that's precisely what the rich and famous Coco Chanel would say of her father. This was not only because a little girl's dreams die hard, but also because her mother could surely not have died for a man who was not worthy of it.

Stricken by tuberculosis and, more importantly, by a lack of love, Jeanne would die a slow death in front of her scared children and an indifferent husband. Even if she could have seen it all coming, she surely could not have escaped it. So it had been from the very start, in Courpière, late in 1880.

That morning, in the market square, the seventeen-year-old Jeanne saw Albert Chanel for the first time. She was immediately taken with him, entering a strange state of shock and awe, and it was him that she obstinately chose, out of all other men. He only had to look at her, his sales patter not even slipping for a moment – already a bad omen. She was heading for disaster yet stubbornly persisted, just as she would stubbornly persist until the day she died.

'My parents were ordinary people, beset by ordinary passions,' Coco often said, in an effort to throw people off with false leads and keep her childhood a secret. In truth, she believed the complete opposite: she admired her mother for having been capable of a love so absolute. As for her father, she would never disavow him or criticize him, even after the events of 1895.

Indeed, what both exasperated and fascinated her about her father was his sense of freedom, which she felt was innate: his way of behaving as if he had no ties and no burdens, running around and pushing at boundaries. She envied him, in a way. If she had been a man, perhaps she would have chosen his travelling profession. Like him, she could have flirted and flattered, sleeping under the stars, and coming back to her family only when she wanted to, not simply because it was her duty.

She believed herself to be the only one who understood Albert Chanel. She knew that he was a poet in his own time, reciting verses on the road between swigs of wine, eyes gazing at the sky. When he came home from his trips, he would tell her stories of splendid golden landscapes, constellations hanging in the sky, fields of grain. He also talked about 'good wheat', a symbol of prosperity and good fortune.[8] As with everything related to her father, Coco would always remember this; she surrounded herself with sheaves of fantastical wheat in bronze, wood and rock crystal, and filled a vase with dried ears of wheat, replacing them every year. She found the same wheat at the Aubazine orphanage; on the coat of arms of her beloved Duke of Westminster, 'azure with a garb or'; and on the gates of her future home in Switzerland. When her friend, Salvador Dalí, offered to paint her something, Coco replied: 'Paint me an ear of wheat.' When she designed her unique 'Bijoux de Diamants' collection of fine jewelry, she chose the theme of constellations: comets and stars like the ones in her father's stories.

She also got her belief in fate from her father, or at least her faith that a path would always lead somewhere, which he called 'luck'. Leaving things up to destiny, letting herself be guided by an invisible hand, that's what Albert taught her as she followed him along the road and they would chat like a father and daughter who wouldn't have a lot of time together.

Coco Chanel, born Gabrielle Chasnel, thought fate lay behind her birth at the Saumur hospice on 19 August 1883, at 4 p.m. on a particularly hot and feverish afternoon. Once again, Albert was absent; worse still, he was in prison in Tours, serving a three-month sentence from 23 June to 23 September 1883, for 'fraud and breach of contract'.[9] He was no stranger to this, for he did not always have the means to pay for the merchandise he ordered. And so it was a woman from the hospice staff who registered the birth of Gabrielle in his stead. The certificate was left unsigned, and the names of her parents were misspelled: 'Henri Chasnel, merchant, aged twenty-eight, and Eugénie Jeanne Devolles, merchant's wife, aged twenty.'

As an adult, Coco never had the document corrected.[10] Although unable to speak to the sequence of cause and effect that led her father to Saumur and her pregnant mother, who already had Julia-Berthe to look after, to follow him, she recognized that there was something mysterious but also intentional there, as if planned from above. As far back as she could remember, she had seen signs everywhere, and this obsession – or rather, this skill – lasted throughout her life.

To Coco, being born in August in an equestrian town like Saumur meant that, from the start, her life had two guardian animals – lions and horses – forming a sort of personal bestiary that she would retain until her death. She used lions as decorative motifs: bronze lions in her living room, lion's heads on suit buttons, stone lions on her gravestone. Horses, on the other hand, remained a living symbol for Coco, who was an excellent rider and a regular at the races.

Strictly speaking, Coco had no memories of Saumur. Try as she might to rack her brain, the earliest images that came to her were from her early childhood in the region of Auvergne: first from Issoire, where she remained until she was five, and then Courpière, where she lived between the ages of five and eleven.

Civil records – certificates of birth, marriage, baptisms, and deaths – and legal records as well as five-yearly censuses[11] fill the gaps in the story that Coco told her close friends. The family lived in Issoire from 1883 to 1888, with a break in 1884 for the wedding of Jeanne and Albert, which was held in Courpière on 17 November 1884. The couple had seven children, four of whom were born on the road, wherever they happened to be. Adrien was born in 1881 in Saintes, Julia-Berthe in 1882 in Aubenas, Coco in 1883 in Saumur, Lucien in 1889 in Guéret. Alphonse and Antoinette were born in Issoire in 1887 and 1889, and Augustin in Courpière in 1891. Two of them, Adrien and Augustin, died during infancy, while Julia-Berthe and Antoinette later took their own lives. Death haunted Coco from a very young age, a recurrent curse that would plague her tragically.

Her maternal grandparents, Gilberte Chardon, a seamstress, and François Devolle, a carpenter, originated from Courpière, where their families had lived for generations. By contrast, her paternal grandparents, Adrien and Virginie Fournier, were travelling market traders from Cévennes who hopped from town to town, leading a nomadic way of life that would later influence Coco. She liked to say that in her family, 'we are born and we die on the road'.[12]

Albert Chanel was born on 19 November 1856, at the Nîmes hospice; he too with an absent father, he too with a misspelled name.[13] He was one of many siblings, the majority of whom died before reaching adulthood. Among his brothers and sisters, two played important roles in the life of Coco Chanel: Adrienne, the future Baroness de Nexon, who, after Julia-Berthe, became Coco's lifelong companion, and Louise, who went on to marry Paul Costier, a railway worker.

CHAPTER 1

Jeanne Devolle lost her mother at the age of six. Her carpenter father remarried and had other children before death took him too. Jeanne and her brother Marin, also a carpenter, were twelve and seventeen, respectively, when they were orphaned. Marin died in Courpière in 1886, aged twenty-eight, at the home of their uncle Augustin Chardon, a gardener.

Coco rarely spoke of Auvergne and her childhood, although, given the slightest opportunity, she would proudly proclaim herself an *Auvergnate* (in fact, she was only half-*Auvergnate*; her father's family were *Cévenole*). A symbolic paradise lost or primordial landscape, it was in this metaphysical Auvergne, this physical and mental land between Courpière and Issoire, that she found something to fuel her adult life. In the meantime, however, she simply observed, imagined, and collected. Her world – a world of dreams – was built around visions, signs, and symbols: her lucky number 5, the horses and lions from her personal bestiary, the ears of wheat and lucky stars from her father's stories. All of these lay beneath the ground, nourishing the roots of her future career.

As an adult, she wandered the landscapes of childhood in her mind. Here were plunging valleys, with streams flowing down; elsewhere were beeches, oaks and firs, wild mushrooms growing by rocky paths; further still, villages on rocky peaks. Approaching Courpière, the landscape grew broader, with clearings like mirages, bright sunlight. And Romanesque churches everywhere.

It was in Courpière that she felt closest to God. While her family thought she was playing outside, she secretly went to pray at the church with a fervour she did not display at Sunday Mass. When she believed she was alone, she had a ritual: entering on the right, through a shadowy recess, she would pause in front of a tomb, then cross the nave diagonally towards the painted wooden Virgin, whose blue colour and sad sweetness she loved.

It was with this same fascination that she watched the work of potters, nailmakers, chandlers, blacksmiths, seamstresses, and weavers. These were artisans of the kind that Coco respected throughout her life, most likely because they taught her to love a job well done, a very Chanel virtue, and also because they were there, busy but present, when her parents were not.

In Issoire, these people were her neighbours, in the lower part of the town by the river, near the mill, outside the old walls. Although it couldn't have been more plain or modest, the family's home on the rue du Moulin-Charrier had the advantage of being open to the four winds and a crossroads, and faced the bridge that led to the city. They lived in the heart of the artisan quarter: that is to say, in the *faubourgs*.

In Courpière, on the other hand, Coco lived in the centre of town on the rue de Minimes with her grand-uncle August Chardon.[14] In that world, the generations were used to all living under the same roof. The Devolle and Chardon families were no exception to the rule; after leaving Issoire, Jeanne and her children moved in with Uncle Augustin and his wife Françoise, who had been alone since the death of their only daughter and the departure of the nephew who had been living with them. Directly opposite stood the Devolle house with its old carpentry workshop.

Nearby, next to the parish close where the nuns lived and her Chardon uncle worked as a gardener, Coco often went to play in a small, abandoned cemetery whose scarce, scattered graves were covered in lichen and weeds. But she felt less at home there than in the other cemetery where her rag doll was laid to rest.

She never returned to her little cemetery after leaving Courpière. Towards the end of 1894, Coco and Julia-Berthe went with their mother to Brive-la-Gaillarde, where once again – one time too many – Jeanne had chosen to follow her husband, who found a job as an innkeeper with his brother Hippolyte. The youngest children, Antoinette, Alphonse and Lucien, remained in Courpière, giving Jeanne some time to settle with her two oldest daughters on the avenue d'Alsace-Lorraine, with a husband who, she believed, had grown tamer.

Early in the morning of 10 February 1895, Coco and Julia-Berthe, aged twelve and thirteen, respectively, were by their mother's bedside as she breathed her last breath. They watched as she choked and spat blood, her death a painful one.[15] Throughout her life, Coco would be haunted by red, the colour of blood, the colour of stained linens and handkerchiefs, the colour that heralded death. She would call it 'that red within us'. She was also haunted by fear of tuberculosis, a disease – or a curse – she believed ran in her family, and would be devastated when her dear André, her 'nephew-son', contracted it. The 'evil disease that comes in through the throat' was a constant source of anxiety and she amassed a collection of scarves to keep it at bay.

Jeanne was just thirty-three when the white sheet was drawn over her face. Typically, Albert was not by her side. The death certificate was signed at nine o'clock in the morning by 'Hippolyte Chanel, wine merchant, aged twenty-three, brother-in-law of the deceased, and Antoine Verdier, tailor, aged thirty-seven'.[16]

On 10 February, devastated yet aware of every detail, Coco could do nothing more than watch. But the worst was yet to come. Suddenly, Albert arrived and shed a few tears in front of the already stiffening body. He drew his two daughters close to him before deciding to inform the family, which in fact meant asking them for help.

Coco later said that they made her father pay for what they blamed on him: Jeanne's painful death. She told André and then Tiny, his daughter, that she 'saw her father begging and pleading'. She would speak of 'the cruel indifference of the family, her inability to stop the abandonment from happening, the boys being placed on farms and the girls being taken to the Aubazine orphanage'.[17]

Gabrielle Maurin, the daughter of Coco's brother Alphonse, confirmed that 'the girls were sent to the orphanage and the boys to live with farmers after their mother died'.[18] This story was corroborated by Adrienne Valet, daughter of Albert Chanel's brother Hippolyte.[19] But no archives from the Aubazine orphanage survive.[20]

So Alphonse and Lucien were sent to farms as 'children of the hospices', while Julia-Berthe, Coco and Antoinette were cared for by family members before being taken to the Aubazine orphanage. They were temporarily housed with Louise Costier, née Chanel, in Varennes-sur-Allier, and with Anaïs Clouvel, née Chardon, in Thiers. By the time of the 1896 census, Coco is recorded as living in Thiers at her aunt Anaïs's home.[21]

The three girls were then entrusted to the nuns of Aubazine (then spelled 'Obazine'), where they would join their young aunt Adrienne, the sister of Albert Chanel, who was attending school there.

Aubazine remained Coco Chanel's painful secret. Speaking of that place would have meant reviving two haunting memories: first, the death of her mother, the pain, the blood, her mother in a coffin, as helpless as she always had been, choked to death by disease and love, having always had to see things to the bitter end; and then, the abandonment that followed, the harshness of her family, the orphanage. Later in life, she spoke of her past freely, with faked confidence, telling multiple versions of the same anecdotes. She only ever truly confided in a few close friends.

Her unhappy childhood was kept inside, but she did sometimes speak about one of the nuns from Aubazine who had mattered to her, because she had always been kind and supportive. It was in memory of this sister, she later said, that she kept a membership card for the Roman Catholic church in her wallet.[22]

When Albert Chanel took his three girls to Aubazine, he told them that he was taking them to an orphanage, but did not say for how long and did not explain why, because he did not know himself. Travelling in a cart with her sisters, drawn by a horse that she had often petted, and often accompanied to the blacksmith's on the outskirts of Courpière with her father, Coco spotted an abbey in the distance: a cold, grey fortress. The closer they got, the colder and greyer the building became. By the time a nun came out to greet them, the little girl felt detached from her own body. From that moment on, everything was a blur, and sounds barely penetrated her ears. 'I'll be back,' Albert said. But his words meant little at that moment: Coco merely registered them mechanically. Later, in the sometimes unbearable silence of the orphanage, she would hear those words echoing inside her, an expression of futile hope.

Then her father departed, his footsteps echoing off the flagstones. As the sound died away, she realized – brutally – that she was alone with her sisters, alone in the world *despite* her sisters.

What saved her that day and kept her from sinking, as Julia-Berthe and Antoinette eventually did, is that, unlike them, Coco retained her faith in her father and chose to believe stubbornly that he was just a victim of circumstance; he was not to blame at all, he loved her and would come looking for her. Unlike her sisters, she was living on a lie, but nonetheless, she lived.[23]

One day she would have to talk about the past, putting an unbearable reality into empty words, so for a long time afterwards, Coco chose to lie. The stories she concocted often changed, even when dictating her memoirs to Louise de Vilmorin, Paul Morand, Michel Déon or Marcel Haedrich.

She imagined a father with whom she was reunited just outside Nîmes, who opened his arms to greet her.[24] She spoke at length about the strict aunts who raised her in Mont-Dore, aunts with whom she lived for ten years – no less – after the death of her mother, a death that Coco would claim had happened when she was six. Amid these fairy tales, she nonetheless found a way to slip in, with a false air of innocence and relative caution that would make it seem like she was merely speaking symbolically, that she dreamed of setting fire to her aunts' barn,[25] as a way not only of divulging her pain but also of expressing in one subtle sentence all of the suppressed hatred she felt towards the relatives who had allowed something unforgivable to happen. 'I knew that Coco was always making up stories,' the journalist Marcel Haedrich said. 'During our years of friendship, I was very much aware that she would recount a different version of her life every day.'[26]

She spent several years with the nuns of Aubazine, years in which she discovered an unexpected strength within herself and built a character that some would consider uncompromising. 'I've survived the worst,' she often said, suggesting she had nothing more to fear. With a proud set of her delicate mouth, she created a way of appearing, her own way of continuing her existence in the eyes of others. She cultivated her inner life, nurturing it with images of a past that she embellished more and more each day. Although, at first, she rejected the cold and severe monastic world she had been plunged into after having her childhood torn from her, she eventually opened up, despite herself, to the Cistercian aesthetic.

She even drew from it a certain idea of beauty that would stay with her for life, a black-and-white starkness, a sense of austerity striving towards absolute purity, the traces of which could be found in what would come to be called 'the Chanel style'. She grew up in a world of perfect proportions, with no useless adornments, where beauty was filtered through the experience of simplicity. She would pray before windows whose purpose was to filter light without telling a figurative story, in front of tracery that hearkened back to monastic discipline and that would one day inspire the double Cs of her signature and her logo. The secret numbers that lay behind the perfectly designed proportions; the sun, the moon and the stars that she saw every day on the tiled floor; the sheaves of wheat displayed in large jars: all of these things became comforting symbols during her childhood.

But despite everything, Coco did not find solace. She never would. Her anger, like a volcano, erupted whenever the topic of family came up. When her poor aunt Louise Costier, with the best of intentions, invited Coco for a holiday at her home in Varennes-sur-Allier, between Vichy and Moulins, the child was nothing a bundle of hatred, a lost little girl, haunted and hunted, who hid herself away in the attic where she spent most of her time reading. Nestled between forgotten trunks and a pile of romance novels, she dreamed of a great love, a love of which only her mother was capable.

Albert Chanel, alas, no longer gave much thought to his children. He continued on his path as a travelling salesman, sometimes opting to have no fixed abode in order to evade the authorities. Traces of him can be found here and there.

In 1898, he was in Issoire, sentenced by the criminal court: 'Albert Chanel, aged forty-two years, salesman, homeless, under prosecution for fraud.' He often had goods sent to the railway station in Issoire, especially imported foodstuffs, and never paid for them. Those who were owed money lodged complaints, but Albert disappeared. The court sentenced him in absentia to one year in prison.[27]

In 1911, he turned up in Quimper, already remarried. According to the census, Albert and Louise, fifteen years his junior, lived in the place Terre-au-Duc and were both shopkeepers.[28] In 1919, his name was included on the marriage certificate of his daughter Antoinette in Paris, but needless to say, he was not present.[29]

When, in 1901, Coco left the Aubazine orphanage for another one in Moulins, she still fantasized, despite being eighteen years old, that her father might come looking for her. Not only did he never come, but she would never see him again.

2
THE LITTLE
YELLOW RING

Moulins, France, 1904. Sundays are often a source of exasperation to Coco, especially the first few sunny Sundays when she observes, fascinated but also annoyed at being so, the elegant women shyly savouring their sorbets or their *La Tentation* pastries before making their way, as the day fades, to the Cours de la Préfecture. As she passes the Sérardy chocolate shop, with its gold and azure shopfront jutting out like the prow of a ship, she shifts her gaze so as not to see the powdered, corseted ladies being presented with boxes of *Palets d'Or* chocolates between greedy giggles. If Adrienne – her young aunt, sister of Albert Chanel and just one year her senior – were not beside her, she would strut through the streets of Moulins in a fury. Instead, she forces herself to stroll with an air of calm, as if nothing were amiss.

But it is precisely this notion of nothing being amiss that is eating at her; she would rather be loud and clear about her contempt for these frivolous women who know nothing about struggle and everything about seduction, as well as speaking, or even shouting, about her own suffering. But as always, Coco refrains and represses, bottling everything inside.

She will keep her head held high; that much she decides. When she makes this promise to herself, dreaming, like her father before her, of a wide world and great deeds, she cannot help but look for a sign – like in the old days – to confirm her convictions. But there's no sign in sight, so all she can do is superstitiously stroke the ring she wears on the little finger of her left hand, an oval citrine mounted point upwards on a gold band – her most prized possession, despite having received it from a stranger.

A few weeks earlier, she had been walking with Adrienne, in the gardens at the foot of the tower known as the Mal-Coiffée (the ruins of the château of the Dukes of Bourbon). It was there that a woman had suddenly appeared; Coco later claimed it was a Roma woman. The woman predicted that Coco's future would have no shortage of men or money. Despite the banal nature of this prediction, Coco seemed so unsettled that the woman slipped her a mysterious object and promised it would bring her good fortune. Then she vanished as quickly as she had arrived. On opening her hand, Coco found what for the rest of her life she would call a 'little yellow ring'. It wasn't worth much, but she would never take it off, even when she was rich and famous, bedecked in the most magnificent jewels, those she bought for herself or those she was given by the Duke of Westminster. She always wore it on the same finger, her left little finger, until it no longer fit and then she began wearing it on a chain, which she kept tucked beneath her blouse. 'I never want to take it off, even in my grave,' she confided towards the end of her life.[30]

Before night fell in Moulins, Adrienne and Coco had a little time to mingle with the locals out promenading on the Cours de la Préfecture, a set of broad landscaped avenues planted with chestnut or lime trees that followed the path of the old city walls. Only when they had no other option, the pair returned to the attic room that they shared on the rue du Pont-Ginguet, in the low-lying districts near the river Allier: a place that could be called the middle of nowhere. It was all they could afford, but at least they had their independence after their years at boarding school (for Adrienne) and in the orphanage (for Coco). With just two beds and a table between whitewashed walls, they were able to make the place pleasant by adding curtains, a tablecloth and bedspreads they made themselves.

The daily walk to the rue de l'Horloge, where they worked as clerks in a women's clothing house, was almost perfectly straight and was not lacking for attractions given that they had to cross the Place d'Allier, with its café terraces, which they could only observe sadly from afar. Although it was small consolation, they liked living near the river. However, to catch a glimpse of the Allier and the Villars garrison on the opposite bank, it was necessary to cling to the narrow window frame and lean out, craning their necks and balancing on their tiptoes.

In town, they often crossed paths with officers of the 10th Chasseurs, who usually hung around in groups, speaking loudly or in low voices, putting on airs, and grand ones at that, well aware of the effect produced by their uniforms and moustaches. Perhaps because they were horsemen, Coco watched them surreptitiously. But out of shyness and even more so out of propriety, she lowered her eyes as soon as they came near. At almost twenty-one, she felt so different from the others that she seemed mysterious and even alluring. Young soldiers were quick to court her. They waited for her at the junction of the rue d'Allier and rue de l'Horloge, on the corner formed by two sides of À Sainte-Marie, formerly the Maison Grampayre, the store where she and Adrienne both worked. But Coco did not so much as glance at them and would walk off haughtily in the opposite direction, savouring the luxury of doing so.

On one particular day, however, she dared to look up and saw a face staring back at her. As if in warning, an image flashed through her mind: it was her parents seeing each other one morning in 1880 in the market square in Courpière. But this did not dissuade her. She felt strangely unassailable, the master of her own destiny, spared from the string of misfortunes that afflicted others, believing she had already lived through the worst. And so she responded to Étienne Balsan (because this was he, the instigator, the first protector, the man without whom nothing would have happened) with a sideways glance, signalling that although she remained on her guard, she was also waiting for his next move.

It was this restraint that ended up captivating Balsan, a soldier doing compulsory military service, a bon vivant, and to top it off, the scion of a rich family of textile industrialists from Châteauroux. Passionate about horses and racing, Balsan was a trainer, owner and jockey, possessing stud farms and a vast property near Compiègne, in La Croix-Saint-Ouen, on the rue Carnot, as well as a former abbey in Royallieu, which had been turned into a holiday home.

As well as her striking, almost androgynous figure and her face that could have belonged to a young lady or a fake ingénue, Coco charmed him with her proud and stubborn attitude. There he was, a seasoned seducer, thrown off guard for the first time and delighted to be so. Coco did not say much, just enough to give him a few glimpses of an embroidered past; once again, there was no mention of the orphanage but of elderly relatives.

She did not mention Aubazine, nor the Notre-Dame boarding school in Moulins, where she had lived alongside Julia-Berthe and Antoinette until a year ago. There she had been reunited with her aunt Adrienne, who was living there as a paying boarder. Coco and her two sisters had not possessed that privilege; instead they had been allowed to enter the part of the school reserved for impoverished girls, known as *la petite école*, which was financed by the wealthiest parents.[31] Crudely cut dresses, second-hand boots, all of these things were a source of shame and made their orphan status painfully obvious.

Coco never forgot this, and spent her whole life promoting a style that gave freedom to women, starting with herself. In fact, it was during her time at Notre-Dame that she discovered an interest in dressmaking, by aptitude and not simply for tradition's sake, like her mother and, before that, her Chardon aunt and the rest of the women in the family. The craft of sewing, as well as the presence of her sisters and Adrienne, somewhat sweetened those last two years of orphanage life. She almost forgot the early days: how her arrival in Moulins had felt like as a second desertion, and how it had been even worse as a self-aware eighteen-year-old.

On that day, she had stood outside a door in a wall so thick that it left no doubt as to what the building was, and looked up at the inscription: 'Notre-Dame Boarding School'. Then she could see nothing but the door, this time closed behind her, and she could finally put a name to what she felt: abandoned. She curled up in the chair offered to her by one of the nuns. Devastated, she told herself she could never live with this loss, with everything having been taken away. At eighteen, she realized that her father would never come to fetch her because she was no longer a little girl.

A few moments – or hours – later, she found herself in the gardens of the boarding school, dazzled, in spite of everything, by the grounds: the sloping lawn, the white buildings with large windows (although she would not live there, the *petite école* being located out by the edge of the grounds), the rows of yellow archways supported by black columns. She felt surprised to still be alive.

It was the nuns who had helped Adrienne and Coco to find jobs at À Sainte-Marie. They started out living in the attic of the clothing house before moving into their room at Pont-Ginguet. Coco's sister Antoinette, who was only sixteen, remained a boarder at Notre-Dame, while Julia-Berthe worked in the market, exhausting herself like their mother, to the point of death.

A child was born in Moulins on 29 November 1904, a child whose given names were André and Marcel, and who would be registered by a man who was not his father: that man's name was Antoine Palasse, a twenty-eight-year-old market trader who lived on the place de la Liberté, just behind the Notre-Dame boarding school. Coco later said that this gentleman 'was paid to acknowledge André'.[32] According to the civil records, the child was Julia-Berthe's, but some doubt remains. André was raised by Coco after the death of her sister and she went to inordinate lengths to help him during the Second World War: he may well have been her own son. But she always wanted to preserve this mystery. Neither André himself nor his daughters, Gabrielle (nicknamed Tiny) and Hélène, ever learned the truth. From the day he was born, he lived with an elderly priest. He always said that his memories of very early childhood were vague and that he could only see the face of that old priest. Coco visited him often before the death of Julia-Berthe. Afterwards, once she got her affairs in order, she came to get him. André was six years old at the time.[33] Many certainly believed that he was her son and not her nephew.[34]

For this to be true, it would mean that Coco was several weeks pregnant at the time of that Sunday scene in the spring of 1904. Even if that were the case, André could not have been the son of Boy Capel, her future great love, as some have claimed.

Now that Julia-Berthe was so often at work in the market, Adrienne replaced her as Coco's steadfast companion. Although she was Albert Chanel's sister – much younger, twenty-six years his junior – Adrienne never talked to her niece about her absent father. Coco deliberately encased herself in the lie about her mythical father who had left for America one morning in 1895. It would have been too loathsome to imagine that her father could have somehow

CHAPTER 2

remained in France, living the same life but with less hope and more bitterness, his eyes no longer dark and proud but drooping half-shut, alcohol staining his lips. A few members of the family heard tidbits about him now and again, before there came a silence so definitive that no one knew what had become of Albert Chanel, assuming he was even still alive.[35]

Coco seemed determined to keep her father's dreams alive. Albert Chanel loved to perform in front of an audience, even if all he was doing was selling hosiery and linens. His daughter, meanwhile, decided to try her luck on stage. It was relatively easy: Moulins, like any self-respecting garrison town, had plenty of cafés and cabarets. She made her debut one evening at La Rotonde, a fashionable *café-chantant* somewhat removed from the main promenades, closer to the train station. The Eastern-inspired pavilion owed its name ('the Rotunda') to its shape, and was set like a cake in the middle of a park, then named the Square de la République. There she performed, among other songs, *Qui qu'a vu Coco?* ('Who has seen Coco?'), a choice that would later be suggested as the origin of her nickname, although it actually predated this period, having come from her father. Her first attempts were relatively promising, not because of her voice but because of her presence. With the boldness only the very shy can display, as well as a fierce desire to 'make it big', she shone on stage when she launched into *Complainte canine* ('The Dog's Lament'), with lyrics that ran:

I have lost my poor Coco,
Coco the dog that I adore,

38

THE LITTLE YELLOW RING

Close to Trocadero,
He'll be far away if he runs more.

Nonetheless, she decided that she would have to take another path if she wanted to become a true success and so force the hand of destiny. To pay tribute to her father and fight back against the cards life had dealt her, she was determined to accomplish some great feat, to gain recognition and perhaps even fame.

In 1906, after temporarily giving up the fashion trade at the age of twenty-three, she went to work in the spa town of Vichy, accompanied by Adrienne. She stayed there for just one season, enough time to explore what seemed, from afar, like a world of possibilities and promise. A photograph shows her sitting on the terrace of 'La Crémerie' in the Nouveau Parc des Sources, an English-style park on the bank of the river Allier. Daydreaming there alongside Adrienne, her gaze lingers on the trees.

Beneath the park's covered arcades, a marvel of decorative metalwork, she crossed paths with the most elegant and exotic of women, who came from every capital of the world. Watching them discreetly and feeling dazzled despite herself, Coco realized, with one of her customary flashes of insight, that she was fascinated by these refined ladies she had always thought she despised. Elated by her discovery, she did not yet know that one day she would become so infatuated with Eastern wisdom as to keep by her bedside a copy of the Bhagavad Gita, one of the most beautiful epic poems of classical India:

The dualities of desire and aversion arise from illusion.
O conqueror of enemies, all living beings in the material
realm are deluded by these.[36]

But patience was not her strong suit. Beneath the blue and
green glass ceiling at the Hall des Sources, Coco was getting
restless at being just a water girl. Her job, paid in tips, consisted
of filling a goblet at one of the hot springs and bringing it to
one of the spa clients. She dreamed of working at one of the
city's many tea houses instead, one decorated in shades of
cream and buttercup and lined with mirrors and gilding, or
perhaps even at the Nouveau Parc, in gallant company. But she
found solace at Vichy's racecourse, where she would go with
Adrienne and their mutual friend, Maud Mazuel, a would-be
socialite unwillingly confined to the role of chaperone, who
lent an air of apparent respectability to the trio. Coco was
already foreshadowing her style revolution by refusing to be
crushed under the weight of huge fancy hats; she also broke
away from the fashions of the era and embraced simplicity,
white collars and small boaters in place of cumbersome gowns.

Near the end of that same year, 1906, Étienne Balsan, who
was still on the scene, made Coco's wildest dreams come true
by asking her to come and stay with him. It was not a new
idea. They had talked about it on several occasions; most
notably when Balsan, who could be romantic when he chose,
had invited her to the Grand Café, the crown jewel of the
Place d'Allier and a dream destination for Coco, who passed
by it every day on the way between the rue du Pont-Ginguet
and the rue de l'Horloge.

When that day came, Coco thought that she had never seen anything so beautiful, but her pride would not let it show. She cast furtive glances at the bevelled mirrors and their endlessly repeating row of receding reflections, and raised her face discreetly towards the wrought iron balcony and the golden yellow light that fell from the glass ceiling, while the whole place resounded with the din, to which she was unaccustomed, of cutlery and chatter. Balsan gallantly pretended not to notice Coco's confusion as she was initiated into the whirl of high society and the joys of luxury with a delight she had not anticipated.

After being disappointed by a father she had spent so long waiting for, Coco found solace in Étienne. Although she was twenty-three, the little girl in her still wanted compensation as well as attention, but this did not prevent her from staying on her guard. Never abandoning herself to passion in order to avoid being abandoned herself: that was her standard procedure. Coco never truly loved Balsan, feeling at best a kind of gratitude tinged with affection towards him. In return, he was entertained and flattered. So he asked her to come home with him, to La Croix-Saint-Ouen, and to Royallieu.

She was delighted, convinced that this new life could, like the wave of a wand, wipe the old one away. Settling into the room set aside for her, spreading her meagre belongings out on the bed, she could not help but feel elated. Her face pressed against the windowpane, she saw a world that, just an hour before, she would not have dared to dream of. Then the euphoria began to fade and a shiver ran through her veins. She realized, much like when a holiday comes to an end, that only the setting had changed, and that she was still herself, cold and alone. The afternoon dragged on, the frivolity of Etienne's merry band of friends seeming almost incongruous, out of place. As evening fell, she rushed back to her room but found no sleep there. Her bouts of sleep-walking, a regular occurrence since the death of her mother, grew more frequent during the first few months of her long stay with Balsan.

She eventually settled in, however, and fell into the routines of the house: reading the morning papers, riding horses, going to the races, dinner parties, pranks and fancy dress. A fun-loving disposition was *de rigueur*, along with a raucous lack of responsibility. A wealthy heir and orphan, Étienne Balsan led his life as he saw fit, inviting to his home or keeping the company of a diverse cast of characters who shared a passion for pleasure. Stars of stage and sport, well-born young men and their mistresses, those were the regulars at Royallieu. They included Émilienne d'Alençon, Gabrielle Dorziat, Jeanne Lery, Suzanne Orlandi, Count Léon de Laborde and Baron Henri Foy.

Coco, who was neither well-born nor an artist, had no special quirks other than her strikingly audacious wardrobe. All that was left was for her to cultivate her own style, one that was deliberately restrained, a clean, lean silhouette that boldly borrowed pieces of men's clothing: trousers, jodhpurs, shirts, ties and bow ties. This was her great invention: to appropriate the male way of dressing and, in so doing, to seize a part of the male prerogative.

With Balsan, she learned to ride a horse but chose to wear jodhpurs and a shirt at a time when women were still wore corsets and rode sidesaddle. Balsan's granddaughter, Quitterie Tempé, recalled that her grandfather 'was shocked and furious to discover that Coco had cut up one of his suits and his favourite shirt to style them her own way.'[37] After these early experiments, Coco started to cross the street to visit the nearest tailor, who was none other than the former tailor for the 5th Regiment of Dragoons of Compiègne. She instructed him to reproduce what she had made when she cut up Balsan's clothes. Thus it was that her style was born. A style that allowed for movement. A style that she created first for herself, then for all women, a kind of 'universal self'.

In this time of inspiration when she was eager to move forward and no longer had the heart to have fun on command or to play at make-believe, something happened that would upend her existence: she fell in love for the first time.

It was on a hunt with hounds in 1908 that she first met Arthur Capel, a friend of Étienne Balsan. She saw him and immediately knew he was the one she'd been waiting for. 'We didn't exchange words, just a look,' she often said. On her return to Royallieu, she met Boy, the nickname given to Arthur Capel by his close friends, and took the terrifying risk – at least for those who have ever been abandoned – of truly loving him; in other words, of loving Boy for who Boy was and not for what Albert Chanel had been.

3

THE CHINESE CABINET

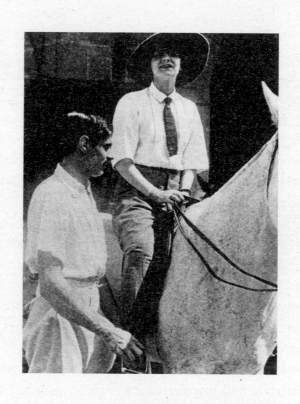

Avenue Gabriel, Paris, France, 1912. She crosses the beige and ivory lounge, looks out the window for a few moments, pensive and light-hearted, nearly forgetting she is waiting for Boy, then goes back to sit among the Coromandel screens and the Eastern furniture: Chinese lacquers and porcelains, sheaves of white tulips in crystal vases. 'How delightful!' the playwright Henry Bernstein had exclaimed the night before when dining there with his wife, before adding, as he made himself comfortable, that the decor resembled its hosts. It is true that Coco and Boy seldom receive visitors, preferring instead to dine out and preserve the sweet intimacy of their immaculate apartment.

Boy already owned this place when he suggested that Coco should join him there. She recalled it happening in the springtime, nearly three years earlier. At the time, Étienne Balsan and Boy each had bachelor flats on the boulevard Malesherbes, and it was at Balsan's place, with his money and his blessing, that Coco, still living in Royallieu, had set up her first millinery workshop. Not only did Balsan finance her early career, but he also helped build up her clientele. The regular guests at Royallieu included prominent *demi-mondaines* and famous actresses such as Gabrielle Dorziat, who was photographed on stage, in fashion magazines and elsewhere wearing Chanel hats. Word of mouth did the rest. Boy paid Coco such frequent visits that their love was soon no longer in doubt to the eyes of others, including Balsan, who sportingly stepped aside while retaining their friendship.

Boy took over the financing of Chanel Modes. But he was thinking bigger and, in 1910, bought Coco a boutique at 21 rue Cambon, a street that would one day become synonymous with her. Then he asked her to come and live with him, not far from there, in his apartment on the avenue Gabriel. She accepted on the condition that she would pay back all the money he fronted her, which she soon did, believing that freedom began with financial independence.

Now approaching thirty, although Coco was as in love as she could possibly have been, she had no thoughts of marriage. Her pride would have never allowed her to be the first to broach the subject with Boy, a subject that also stirred an irrational fear in her. She was aware that the tragic fate of her mother had something to do with it, but what she refused to see behind her inability to commit was the shadow cast by her mythical father. She also believed that there was a price to pay for any great undertaking and that the success she aspired to was bound to come with a certain degree of solitude. She imagined herself as a child again, on her knees in the church in Courpière, asking God to bestow a special talent upon her, to which she promised to devote her life.

While she was not Mrs Arthur Capel, she was nevertheless received as a guest on Boy's arm in Royallieu at the home of Étienne Balsan, who clearly held no grudges. She was also entrusted with the task of creating costumes for a 'country wedding', one of the many fancy-dress parties that so delighted the estate's regulars. She herself dressed as the best man – a little jacket, a white shirt and an ascot – looking strikingly androgynous, while Boy Capel became the mother-in-law, alluring despite his full skirts and the nest of ribbons on his head.

Like so many other women, Coco was bowled over by the charm of Boy Capel, his thick black hair and the proud way he stood. English on his father's side, French on his mother's, Arthur Edward Capel was born in Brighton, Sussex, in 1881. He was the son of Arthur Joseph Capel, a man from a modest background who had made his fortune through hard graft in the shipping business, and of Berthe Lorin, a Parisian his father had met in London and who died at the age of forty-six when Boy was twenty-one. He had been sent to the prestigious Beaumont College in Old Windsor, Berkshire, a sort of Catholic version of Eton where Coco's nephew André Palasse would one day study.

Following in his father's footsteps, Boy was a shipowner and travelled frequently not only between London and Paris but also to the USA, North Africa and Asia. Just like his father, he was highly ambitious and thirsty for recognition. He delighted in one rumour, which was untrue yet persistent: that he was the natural son of one of the Péreire brothers, a renowned banking family. This made him feel as though he belonged to a lineage of conquering heroes who were the bastard sons of kings or gods and who, through their actions, forged a certain kind of immortality. Eager to make his way in the world, he juggled mistresses and did not burden himself with principles.

Engaged throughout his life in a sincere spiritual and philosophical quest, Boy was rather more than Paul Morand made him out to be in the fictionalized portrait that appeared in Morand's novel *Lewis and Irene*, which bore the following dedication: 'For Coco Chanel, this Lewis who was just a little bit Boy Capel'. Lewis, the character based on Boy, is described in the book as a 'bold iconoclast with his ill-breeding, vanity and the haphazard methods of a financial dabbler', who 'only knew Europe from having travelled through it on business, often imperfectly, always hurriedly, without ever opening either his eyes or his heart to it.' And later: 'He did not believe in too much self-examination. Neither pride nor personal integrity mattered to him, as he always acted on impulse. His reflexes stood him in the stead of morals and education.'[38]

True, Boy was a busy man, a fighter, a sportsman (a champion polo player), a shrewd businessman, and a future liaison officer for Clemenceau, both officially and unofficially, during the Great War. But he was also a seeker of spirituality, fascinated by Hinduism, a Theosophist, an avid reader with a love of sacred texts as well as political works, Voltaire and Nietzsche. He was a man of intuition who relied, like Coco, on signs and symbolism, who could see into people's souls and perceive their hidden wounds.

Despite some grievances – his long absences, the mistresses she was aware of – Coco felt loved for the first time, with a patience that was nothing like the patience of her mother, who was submissive and resigned, but the patience of a woman who was respected for what she was, with her desire for independence and her awareness of her unique destiny. It was precisely because she felt so loved that the miracle happened. Boy encouraged her to embark on her own path, to be daring, to embrace freedom and boldness in all their rawness, qualities she would always retain. The foundations for a great business were laid, but neither Coco nor Boy suspected that this was to be the beginning of a future empire.

In Deauville, while savouring their last carefree summer – the summer of 1912 – Boy leased a boutique on the rue Gontaut-Biron, between the brand-new façades of the casino and the Hôtel Normandy. As in Paris, Coco became a milliner, but the shop sign now displayed her full name – 'GABRIELLE CHANEL' – emblazoned in capital letters across a pale awning with subtle stripes. The boutique was never empty, especially as the couple became, via the pencil of the caricaturist Sem, one of the most prominent of their day. In a now-famous caricature, Boy is depicted as a centaur, wearing a polo helmet and brandishing a hat on the end of his mallet. Pressed up against him is a young woman – Coco Chanel, of course.

Adrienne and Antoinette came to join them in Deauville and acted as models, parading around in Gabrielle Chanel hats, which made heads turn with their striking yet elegant simplicity. With a burst of energy from this success, Coco expanded beyond hats, soon designing accessories and then flowing and loose-fitting garments. The clothes combined comfort, simplicity and femininity – her cornerstones

– and were admirably modelled by her two muses: her aunt Adrienne and her sister Antoinette.

Their presence, however, could not ease Coco's deep grief. Three years earlier, in 1910, Julia-Berthe, her sister and first playmate, had died. When Coco heard the news, she had fallen apart, heartbroken to learn that her sister had taken her own life. In later years, she often spoke to André and his daughter, Tiny, about Julia-Berthe's wish to 'end her days by rolling in the snow until she died from cold'. Coco preferred this version of the story, even though she was well aware that Julia-Berthe had died in the month of May since she had organized the ceremony and burial in the Parisian cemetery of La Chapelle.[39]

Perhaps Coco was too preoccupied by the deaths of those close to her – her brothers who passed away at a young age, her mother, then Julia-Berthe – to face those caused by the war. In the summer of 1914, while Deauville was emptying out, she followed the advice of Boy, now enlisted, who suggested 'not closing the boutique, staying there and waiting'. She obeyed on pure survival instinct, and did not try to donate her time or visit the wounded. It was too tough for someone still struggling with her own grief and with the ghosts who would not leave her in peace.

Her brother Alphonse, also enlisted, asked her to provide for the needs of his pregnant partner, who was not the wife he had married four years earlier. Throughout her life, Coco did not hesitate to come to the aid of her friends, to support her family, to send comfortable allowances; throughout her life, she would pay, over and over again.

Tired of pacing the apartment on the avenue Gabriel, Coco sinks into her beige sofa, the legendary seat where she will one day receive Paris's high society. A deep sense of anxiety makes her doubt whether Boy will ever return. The nagging worry feels like a cruel re-enactment of scenes from her childhood; the little girl waiting for her father and then finally flinging her arms around his neck, before being given a gift, the inevitable gift that solved nothing. Boy, frequently away in London and sometimes off to more distant lands, regularly brings gifts too: a piece of furniture, a trinket, a book, a pearl necklace. The latest is a Chinese wedding cabinet in a deep, brownish red shade, which Coco decides to keep empty out of superstition. As with everything of Boy's that she kept, she considered this piece as one of her most prized possessions and, in the twilight of her life, gifted it to Tiny.

When Boy finally appears, he finds her reading the Bhagavad Gita, apparently open to Chapter III, and the most heavily annotated pages:

Therefore, giving up attachment, perform actions as a matter of duty because by working without being attached to the fruits, one attains the Supreme.[40]

The book was Boy's own copy, given to her as a token of affection, the copy he himself had annotated, on which he had meditated. Coco could see that there was something fundamental there, the key to the peace she could not find, although she could not explain it. Any interest in Hinduism she possessed was because it echoed her inner world, the childhood world of symbols, superstitions and secret prayers.

She imagined Boy finding his way through the fog where ordinary mortals get lost, marching straight ahead and knowing where his steps were leading him. She would have liked to believe him when he claimed that one can serve God by pursuing one's own interests; all she dreamed of was for his profound convictions to match his everyday actions. But for now she was assailed by doubt.

In the last few weeks of peace, early in the summer of 1914, she had started to gain recognition no longer only as a milliner but as a *couturière*, attracting a wealthy clientele, including the influential Baroness Rothschild. By the middle of the war, her business was booming to such an extent that even the great couturier Paul Poiret was getting nervous. But she could not celebrate; it felt wrong to be dressing these elegant fashion-hungry women, hiding away in their Normandy villas, while knowing of the scale of the devastation, the blood-soaked soil and the bodies gutted by shells.

One day, when her self-examination felt like gazing into a bubbling cauldron of guilt, Boy's words awakened other echoes within her. Suddenly, her goal became clear, like a minor revelation: it was to create modernity. Fate, which until that moment had brought nothing but raw pain, was finally offering her her first chance, a chance she seized on shrewdly, with no self-deception or misplaced heroism, refusing to feign compassion. 'One world was ending, another was about to be born. I was in the right place; an opportunity beckoned, I took it. I had grown up with this new century: I was therefore the one to be consulted about its sartorial style.... True success is inevitable,' she later said.[41]

Her ascension continued as it had started: she went where the winds and the roads took her, much as Albert Chanel had done. In the summer of 1915, Boy invited her to join him in Biarritz when he had a few days of leave, and she opened a new boutique there – her first couture house – with the encouragement of her companion, who was always quick to detect a good business opportunity; here, it took the form of a wealthy Spanish clientele.

As she followed her intuition and drew inspiration from her personal style, she foreshadowed the emancipation of women. She got rid of tight waists and did away with corsets, continuing what Poiret had timidly begun: she shortened dresses and freed the body, favouring movement and comfort. She embraced jersey, reserved up until then for men's undergarments, buying up a supply that the fabric manufacturer Rodier had feared could not be sold. She remained loyal to this flexible fabric throughout her life.

In 1916, her striking 'chemise dress', with its deep V-neck, was hailed by the American press, with the magazine *Harper's Bazaar* depicting it in an illustration. Also in 1916, she designed a long *marinière* in ivory silk jersey with a full body, a sailor's collar and no fitted darts, allowing for movement. She wore it belted with a simple flowing sash.

During this period, Coco employed several hundred workers scattered between Paris, Deauville and Biarritz and was finally able to repay the entirety of the money loaned to her by Boy. She had succeeded in buying her freedom and independence through hard work.

Boy himself also saw his business prosper. But he was not content just to make a fortune; he had political aspirations and, unfortunately for Coco, social ambitions too. By 1917, he was often away in London. After all, he was a liaison officer highly valued by Clemenceau.

When they did meet in Paris, Boy took her to talks given by Isabelle Mallet at the Theosophical Society. Strangely, Coco found this world of magic, poetry and symbols to be quite familiar. Long afterwards, she remembered the lecture on 'the religious idea of sacrifice', given on the day of the full moon in April 1917, or the readings of Indian poetry, given her lasting belief that poets were true instigators, able to unravel the mysteries of the world.

She would follow Boy anywhere, probably because he never asked her to. She loved him all the more because they shared the same ideas about freedom. But what she sensed, and what made her anxious, was that he would always be driven by his ambition and his desire for status rather than by his feelings.

This realization hit her like a slap, one May evening in 1917 as she was dressing for the Opera in their apartment on the avenue Gabriel. Shaking, she grabbed a pair of scissors, and thought about those she had lost or buried, and about Boy, swearing to love him 'till death comes'; she repeated this phrase, which was painful, given how much she still loved her mother, and began to hack feverishly at her hair, clutching the dressing table to hold herself steady. Her long brown braid slithered to the ground, coiling on the floor like a snake. Later she told a far-fetched story about a boiler that had exploded, forcing her to cut off her hair before leaving for the Opera. But in private, she called it 'a sacrifice for Boy'.[42]

She had started a fashion. The actress Cécile Sorel and the singer Martha Davelli, Mrs Letellier (wife of the powerful owner of *Le Journal*, a Paris newspaper) followed in her footsteps. Some people turn everything they touch into gold: Coco turned everything she did into fashion, revolution, emancipation.

The year 1917 was also when Boy, who was spending more time at his Chelsea flat than in Paris, published the book *Reflections on Victory and a Project for the Federations of Governments*, a bold book that was European before its time. It was praised in the *Times Literary Supplement* and became the talk of London, helping to establish its author's political ambitions.

While Boy's ascension was seemingly irresistible and aristocratic young widows were becoming interested in him, Coco sought out a dizzying array of distractions. She frequented dinner parties, became a 'character', met Misia Sert – a great patron of the arts who would become a close friend – and masterfully managed her businesses in Paris, Deauville and Biarritz, while emanating a self-confidence that made her dazzling.

It was while living this life that, a few months later, she was struck down in mid-flight by the news that Boy had married another woman, Diana Lister, the daughter of a lord. She had suspected this would happen, that he would stubbornly

choose a woman with a title, but she had not expected it to hit her so hard, given how much she had already accomplished. She picked herself up, however, as she always did, continuing to tell herself that there was another fate waiting for her, a fate far more glorious than that of a wife or a kept woman.

Besides, nothing changed after the wedding. Boy continued to come and go between London and Paris; Coco continued to love him from afar, and welcome him back with joy. Her pride would not allow to her to admit that the joy was tainted with bitterness. Her pride also led her to rent a home of her own, La Milanaise, in Garches. Noticing that she was doing well without him, Boy paid her regular visits, which became even more frequent and passionate at the end of the war, after the birth of his first daughter.

With peace restored, Coco left 21 rue Cambon for number 31 in the same street, triumphantly taking her place as a *couturière*. Soon afterwards, Boy found her far less available, busy with preparations for her sister Antoinette's wedding, as busy as if it had been her own. In addition to the wedding gown, Coco designed the wardrobe that her sister would take with her to Canada. On 11 November 1919, not far from the rue Cambon in the town hall of the 8th *arrondissement*, in the presence of Arthur Capel and Maurice de Nexon (Adrienne's fiancé, whom she would not marry until 1930), Antoinette wed Oscar Edward, a Canadian ten years her senior, before leaving for Ontario with him.

After this departure, Coco and Boy enjoyed a second honeymoon phase. Except, of course, that Boy's lawful wife was waiting back in London, pregnant with their second child. Shortly before Christmas, Boy managed to slip away with the excuse that he had some business in Paris. With their meeting having been postponed for so long, he was even happier to see Coco, and was reluctant to leave her to join his family on holiday in Cannes. Neither Coco, who gave him a final kiss on the front steps of La Milanaise, nor his wife and daughter, who were waiting for him in Cannes, would ever see Boy again.

It was Léon de Laborde who came in the middle of the night to deliver the terrible news to Coco. He told her that Boy's automobile, thrown off balance by a burst tyre, had gone off the road near Fréjus. But as he described the fatal accident, Coco's ears began ringing and she could no longer hear his words. When she finally realized what had happened, the scream she let out resounded throughout the entire house. She then demanded to be taken to the site of the accident as quickly as possible, refusing to wait until daybreak.

Arriving the next day after an exhausting, silent journey, she saw the wreck on the roadside, recognized the car and began to sob. She wept for Boy, and also for herself, who had, yet again, lost everything, crouching like a little girl, a frail figure in mourning.

When she asked to see the body, they told her he had already been laid in his coffin in Fréjus, with military honours. All she could do was imagine, which may have been even worse. She couldn't help seeing him, that body dug out from the twisted metal, that face, blood-soaked and unrecognizable. And it was against those things that she raged – although she said nothing out loud – the brutality of death, obscene and sudden, and her beautiful Boy, mutilated. She learned that his death had come on 22 December 1919, 'at two in the afternoon',[43] as if Boy, who loved the number 2 so much, had himself chosen the hour and the date to stop the clock. He was thirty-seven years old. Coco was two years younger.

In her grief, she thought of Boy's books, of his belief in reincarnation, of death occurring because, deep down, we want to put an end to this life and move on to the next. For a few moments, her pain eased. When it returned, Coco began to choke, thinking that she was coughing up blood, but when she looked in disbelief at her handkerchief, it was spotless. Much later, she said: 'I had a choice: die or pursue what I had built with Boy.'[44]

Until the end of her days, she would be incapable of lightheartedness during the Christmas celebrations. And until the end of her days, she continued to recreate the decor from the days of her first love, the Coromandel screens and the furniture and artworks from the East, in all her homes.

4

THE BROWN
LEATHER WALLET

Venice, Italy, 1920. She wanders grief-stricken in the harsh light by the Grand Canal. She sees nothing but water all around, stagnant and dark, all-enveloping. She walks with shoulders hunched, steps hurried, eyes fixed on the ground; she recognizes herself in the damp cobblestones and eroded stonework, the choking tangle of canals. Suddenly, a white building appears, stopping her in her tracks at the place where the Punta della Dogana merges with the horizon. She could have fallen to her knees, but she settles for sitting on the steps. And it is only then and there that she notices the curves and the volutes – sources of comfort – and the dome that crowns the church.

Entering Santa Maria della Salute, she allows herself to cry softly, just as she did in days gone by, in the church of Courpière when she knew she was all alone. She could not care less about the visitors stealing glances at her. Hands together, face wet with tears in the light of the votive candles, she prays for so long that the words grow clear. 'Thy will be done', she whispers. Forgetting her anger and her sadness, in a moment of grace that she will never know again, Coco embraces life for the first time.

She made a vow to hold onto a symbol of this brief, shining moment. The same day, she bought a brown leather wallet and, over the years, used it to collect holy pictures: Mother Teresa, St Agatha, the Madonna of the Olives, 'Blessed Pierre Louis Marie Chanel, missionary of the Society of Mary and first martyr of Oceania (1803–1841)', whom she mistakenly thought to be her ancestor. It also held a card printed and signed by her that read: 'I declare my adherence to the Roman Catholic faith. In the event of a serious accident or emergency transport to a hospital, I call for a Catholic priest by my side. If I die, I wish for the prayers of the Catholic Church. This is my formal will. Being of sound mind, I demand its enactment. Gabrielle Chanel, 31, rue Cambon, Paris.'

She kept this wallet with her from that moment onwards. It later held family photographs: André, of course, and sometimes his grandsons, Guillaume and Pierre-Hugues, the children of Tiny.[45]

She later said that Misia Sert saved her, but it was mostly La Salute, Venice's famous church, that pried her from the grip of death, from the sickness of despair, from the endless grief that stripped everything of meaning, including her own existence. 'Die or pursue what I had built with Boy.' She had been repeating these words on her knees in the house of God when it suddenly struck her: she had to live.

In the months that followed 22 December 1919, Misia had indeed tried everything she could think of to help the numb and haggard Coco. She dragged Coco to the parties and balls she had been invited to, declaring that the woman seen as little more than a 'saleswoman' by high society was her friend. Thanks in part to Coco's melancholy charm, it did not take long for the salon doors to open to her on their own. But

Coco continued to languish. 'I tried desperately to think of ways to distract her,' Misia said.[46] Shortly after marrying the painter José María Sert, she offered to take Coco to Venice, where, Misia believed, Coco might be brought back to life.

However, what struck Coco from the moment she arrived was the decay: the slow anguish, the gradual sinking, the constant delaying of death, the stagnant water. It was only later than she allowed herself to be charmed by the unpredictable light of Venice, glittering and effusive. She began to enjoy her solitary walks: with the exultation of an explorer, she would lose herself in the labyrinth of alleyways and closely packed houses. Around the bend of a street or a bridge, she might stumble upon an unexpected square, a sleepy palazzo in morning mists, a vegetable garden behind a low wall. On sleepless nights, she would glide to the balcony to listen, for hours on end, to the voices, to the whistling and lapping of a Venice she was learning to love.

Finally, one day, while Misia, as usual, lazed in bed, refusing to leave the house so early, Coco and Sert disappeared into Venice together. Short and stocky in stature, Sert was a painter of huge frescoes, an eccentric and baroque character who was more than a guide for Coco: he played a key role in her aesthetic education. She followed him from museum to museum, listening eagerly to his lectures on Tintoretto, Titian, Longhi and Guardi, noticing the details of a frieze, a mosaic, a capital, or a rose window, the symbolic lions of Venice depicted a thousand times in marble, stone or bronze. She learned to distinguish between Venice's many artistic styles and genres, being delighted by the city's Byzantine splendour and pondering the concept of beauty; she was already more interested in the pursuit of perfection than the creative act itself. Then they stopped at the Caffè Florian to meet up with Misia and enjoy the wood panelling, rich upholstery and literary atmosphere. When evening fell, the three dined lavishly, at the expense of José María Sert, who demanded that every supper was sumptuous and washed down with rare wines.

José María Sert was Misia's third husband, following Thadée Natanson, founder of *La Revue blanche* and surrounded by a circle of painters, musicians and writers, and then Alfred Edwards, the wealthy tycoon who owned the newspaper *Le Matin* and the Théâtre de Paris. José María was also the most exuberant, the most flamboyant of the three. Misia couldn't help loving this man who was so much like her, she who had been the muse and model for many great names: Vuillard, Bonnard, Toulouse-Lautrec, Renoir. Misia had always lived among artists, after all: as the daughter of the Polish sculptor Cyprien Godebski – a tireless worker with a certain romantic love of beauty – she had, as a child, played the piano on the knees of Franz Liszt before taking lessons with Gabriel Fauré.

At the time that Coco first met Misia and José María Sert (who was not yet her husband), at a dinner party at Cécile Sorel's house in 1917, Misia knew every prominent Paris artist. At forty-five years old (born in 1872 in St Petersburg), with pale shoulders and plump arms, she was resplendent, and no stranger to the gaze of painters. She was one of those sensual women who would grasp the hand of the person they were talking to, one of those brilliant women who could not bear to be contradicted, let alone outshone by another woman.

Coco, slight and inconspicuous, hardly seemed like a potential rival. But Misia sensed a power hidden within her, and that is what intrigued her. 'At table, my attention was immediately drawn to a very dark-haired young woman. Despite the fact that she did not say a word, she radiated a charm I found irresistible.'[47] She made sure, therefore, during that first evening, to sit next to Coco and, the next day, rushed to the rue Cambon to see her again, so taken was she. Misia was unpredictable but determined when she wanted something. Coco, who would have been wary of such zeal on the part of a man, was delighted to attract the friendship of such an unusual woman.

Two days later, she answered Misia's invitation and went to see her in her apartment at 29 quai Voltaire. Although she usually loathed piles of dusty objects and often said that 'an interior is the natural projection of the soul', Coco was not put off by the bric-à-brac that Misia surrounded herself with: blue pinned butterflies, fans in glass cases, mother-of-pearl trinkets, crystal and lacquerwork.

Coco and Misia forged an exclusive, passionate friendship: stormy but loyal. Until death parted them, they supported each other through the worst of times, although they could be ruthless during the best. The toughness they shared came from their early years. Misia, like Coco, never truly healed from her childhood wounds. Her mother had died in childbirth, exhausted after chasing her fickle husband to Russia, where he had met a new woman, 'Aunt Olga', who was also pregnant. The motherless Misia was raised by this surrogate until the day her father fled, lured away by a rich Polish widow.

The paths of Coco and Misia were so similar – scarred by abandonment and death, as well as by suicide, and most of all by heartbreak – that their meeting seemed inevitable, just as it was inevitable that their friendship would be turbulent, fuelled by quarrels and reconciliations.

The exuberant Misia and the more reserved Coco (she was not naturally so, but she would generally take a step back when in the company of her friend), shared a rare ability to enjoy the present moment, intensely, as if it were their last, knowing the value of life better than anyone. Their presence was therefore sought after, especially in the artistic circles in which they were viewed as muses and, at times, also played the role of patrons.

A cohort of artists gravitated around them, including Pablo Picasso, Jean Cocteau, Paul Morand, Igor Stravinsky and Sergei Diaghilev, who was the director of the Ballets Russes as well as a contemporary of Misia and a longtime friend. Coco hosted them at Bel Respiro, a beige roughcast villa perched on the hill in Garches, at the junction of the rue Alphonse-de-Neuville and the rue Édouard-Detaille, where she had settled shortly after Boy's death. Boy had bought the villa for his wife and himself a year before he died.[48] Coco had the shutters painted black – an extravagance in the eyes of the locals – as a public expression of her mourning.

The writer Henry Bernstein, whom she knew from her time on the avenue Gabriel, lived in the house next door with his wife Antoinette and her daughter. In a photograph taken on a street in Garches, the daughter can be seen holding the hand of Coco, who is dressed in a cape and smiling under her cloche hat.

In 1920, she took a suite at the Ritz to free up her home for Igor Stravinsky and his family. For almost two years, Bel Respiro rang with the sound of the piano, brought to life by the maestro's inspiration. When he moved out, Stravinsky, as a gesture of deep gratitude, gave Coco the gift of an icon painting, the most precious possession he had brought with him from Russia: a symbol of his exile. Coco would keep this icon on her bedside table for the rest of her life.

It was in the same period that Coco gave a cheque to Sergei Diaghilev, despondent at not being able to stage a revival of *The Rite of Spring*. In the words of Boris Kochno, the young Ukrainian poet and secretary to Diaghilev, this cheque 'exceeded his highest expectations'. In return, Coco asked for the utmost discretion regarding her gesture, mostly to avoid upsetting Misia but also to avoid having to explain herself.

Venice had transformed her. Not only had she rediscovered her love of life, enough to open herself up to others, but she had also learned to believe in herself, to put her aesthetic ideas into words. Alternating between fanatical work and society events mean drawing on an unusually deep well of energy. But she was not fooling herself. She was well aware that she was running away from her own truth, from the pain in which her sisters had drowned.

After Julia-Berthe in 1910, Coco learned that Antoinette had also taken her own life on 2 May 1921. How she did it is unknown, but what is certain is that she had been unhappy in Ontario and that, less than a year after her wedding, she fled to Buenos Aires with a man who was not her husband. It was there that she had died, under circumstances that left no doubt in the minds of those close to her. The sole survivor of the Aubazine trio, Coco now had to face the guilt of having outlived her two tragic sisters.

But she did not have to bear this hardship alone. Grand Duke Dmitri Pavlovich, whom she had met in Paris, offered her, if not a shoulder to cry on, then a compassionate ear. There was something of the anxious, lonely child in him, which moved Coco even before he had uttered a word. He too had lost his mother, but at birth. He had subsequently been raised by stern governesses before, at the age of eleven – nearly the same age as Coco when her own tragedy had struck – being separated from his father, Grand Duke Paul, who had been banished by Tsar Nicolas II for having remarried against his wishes. Years later, at the age of twenty-five, Dmitri had been, alongside Prince Youssoupov, one of the instigators in the assassination of Rasputin, which had resulted in his exile and, consequently, his escape from the Russian Revolution. At the age of twenty-nine, free but bruised, with heroic blond looks that seemed romantic yet stoic, he met Coco, eight years his senior, in Biarritz, where many White Russians gathered, survivors of a bygone world. As if dazed, she let herself be charmed by this Russian soul. That innate awareness of ephemerality and the closeness of death, of honour, splendour and magnificence, that particular way of embracing excess without becoming its slave, those nights that never ended, drinking vodka while brimming with tears: everything was mesmerizing to her.

The house of Chanel was also running on Russian time. Penniless princesses and countesses, beautiful and distinguished young women were hired as embroiderers, shop assistants and models. Although she retained her quintessential restrained style, Coco enhanced her collections with Russian-inspired motifs, including long belted blouses reminiscent of those of Russian peasants, as well as embroidered dresses and coats. In fact, the demand became such that she entrusted the embroidery workshop to Grand Duchess Maria, the sister of Dmitri. No one would ever see so many furs at the rue Cambon as during those years.

Grand Duke Dmitri was not merely an inspiration for Coco (as Boy Capel had been and as the Duke of Westminster would be); he also unwittingly helped her to make her fortune. En route to Monte Carlo, the pair made a stop in Grasse, where Dmitri introduced her to Ernest Beaux, a perfumer who had formerly lived in Moscow. It was from this meeting that Chanel N°5 was born.

Coco knew exactly what she was looking for. The fragrances of the era were representational, like jasmine, rose or lily of the valley; they evoked the familiar. What she wanted was the opposite: she imagined a fragrance that emanated mystery, something refined and absolute, a feminine abstraction, 'a perfume for a woman with the scent of a woman,' she said.[49]

Ernest Beaux presented her with two series of samples, numbered from 1 to 5 and from 20 to 24. She liked 22, which she would put on the market a year later in 1922, but number 5 was her first choice. Quite naturally, she named it N°5: the number that had been her favourite since childhood; the number that, as a little girl, she scratched into the earth with a fallen twig; the number that she would playfully seek out amid the dates carved on the gravestones in the Courpière cemetery; the number that she would keep finding throughout her entire life, as though it were always with her.

She never wondered why she was so fond of the number 5 with its serpent-like shape. At least, not until she heard Boy talk about the five-headed deities of Hinduism, the five levels of the soul, the five kinds of vision in Buddhism, the significance of the number 5 in China, and in alchemy, and many other facets of this sacred and magical number. For her whole life – and even beyond, for she chose to decorate her own tomb with five stone lions – 5 was Coco's number, her lucky number when gambling, and the date she chose to present her collections, which were generally launched on 5 February or 5 August. Chanel N°5, meanwhile, was officially launched in 1921, at 31 rue Cambon.

Its name was as modern as its complex formula – with some eighty ingredients, most of them expensive, including Grasse jasmine and rosa centifolia. The bottle too was almost pharmaceutical in its simplicity, a modernist statement in an era of abundant ornamentation. It was also transparent because, Coco explained, 'it is the contents that are essential'. Could she have ever dreamed that this perfume would one day be displayed at the Museum of Modern Art in New York?

In her home, N°5 flowed in abundance. She did not use the fragrance in moderation: she loved it so much that she sprayed it on her clothes, around her rooms, and even into her fireplaces. When she came to the rue Cambon, the staff would spray N°5 on the staircase to greet her.

N°5 was such a success that it made Coco's fortune. But contrary to popular belief, although she had business sense and came from the Auvergne region, which had a reputation for penny-pinching, she was not a flawless businesswoman. In truth, the commercial minutiae bored her, and she preferred to leave others in charge of the details. Several years later, she co-founded the Société des Parfums Chanel with brothers Pierre and Paul Wertheimer, who also owned the firm of Bourjois. With a factory in Pantin (just outside Paris), and another in New York, these captains of industry had considerable firepower. It was Théophile Bader, a mutual friend and the owner of Galeries Lafayette, who introduced them to Coco at the races in Deauville, and they got along wonderfully well. The company was founded on 4 April 1924: Coco was allocated 10 % of the capital, Théophile Bader, who would distribute the perfumes, 20 %, and the Wertheimers, who would produce the perfumes and take on all the risk, 70 %.

After being used for the first time in 1921, on the stopper of the N°5 bottle, the double C logo was printed on the 1924 sales catalogue for Parfums Chanel. Symbols from Coco's childhood were gradually permeating her creative realm.

She believed that she owed everything to Boy: her meeting with Grand Duke Dmitri, then with Ernest Beaux; the fragrance she had dreamed of, presented to her as if by magic

and which seemed less like a perfume and more like a quin-
tessence, a mysterious elixir; and last of all, the number 5,
which had been assigned to her by the great beyond.

Shortly after Boy's death, someone had come to see her,
a Hindu gentleman who introduced himself as a friend of
Boy and who had played polo on the same team as him. She
never forgot his visit, nor his words to her: 'We must go on
living,' he had said, before proving his good faith by telling an
anecdote that only Coco and Boy could have known about.
She firmly believed that, on that day, it had been Boy coming
to speak to her from the other side. And soon, she believed,
she would no longer need an intermediary to speak with the
dead: her mother, Julia-Berthe, Antoinette, Boy.

Perhaps it was this love of magic and the occult, and
poetry too, that stopped Coco from becoming intoxicated by
fame, and by the enticements and comforts of high society.
Her brief affair with the Great Duke Dmitri soon came to an
end. In 1926, he married a wealthy American heiress, Audrey
Emery, in Biarritz. But Coco, incapable of final goodbyes,
maintained a friendship with him until his death in 1942.

5
THE POET'S MANUSCRIPT

Faubourg-Saint-Honoré, Paris, France, 1924. She sits in a garden chair at the foot of the tall trees, planted in such close rows that the walls of the property can barely be seen, let alone the avenue Gabriel that lies beyond the broad lawn. It was this enclosed garden, even more so than the sumptuous salons, the wood panelling and the adjoining rooms, that persuaded her to rent the ground floor and the first floor of the Hôtel Rohan-Montbazon at 29 rue du Faubourg-Saint-Honoré, although it was also a far more prestigious address than her old home in Garches.

She savours a few moments of calm before the onslaught of visitors. As is her habit in these situations, she holds a book in her hand: a collection of poems on which to meditate. She could recite them with her eyes closed, as well as the dedication, which she contentedly recalls: 'With my whole heart until its last beat –P.' She was seated in the same spot, she remembers, when Pierre Reverdy, the poet, the only man she would truly love after Boy, gave her *Les Épaves du ciel*, his most recent manuscript.

It was Misia Sert who had introduced them four years earlier, after Boy's death. Coco and Reverdy stood in astonishment, like two lost friends reunited. He had been particularly struck, not by the elegant slender figure draped in jewelry but by her sparkling gaze, unblinking beneath a tilted hat. He immediately sensed the sadness within her, an intimacy with death, a restrained sincerity, a justified mistrust. On her side, Coco had felt his bond with a rocky region filled with sunshine and a rugged, rural childhood that reminded her of her own.

On the day they first met, Misia had, as usual, monopolized the poet's attention. It is true that she was one of his most fervent admirers and most dogged supporters, even rallying readers to buy the magazine *Nord-Sud*,[50] a lost cause given that the publication would not survive for long. In 1922, a grateful Reverdy had signed a copy of *Cravates de chanvre* illustrated with prints by Picasso: 'To my dear friend Misia, let this be a token of my admiration, of my profound and respectful affection.'

With Coco, on the other hand, the sense of closeness took precedence over admiration because, perhaps unusually, Coco the couturière and Reverdy the poet were united by certain fundamental beliefs: the eternal nature of the quest; imagination as a vital recourse; reality as a thing to be overcome and not seized head-on. They soon realized that what they had taken to be friendship was actually love, furious and passionate.

Reverdy, like a lost butterfly, fluttered around the apartment on the rue du Faubourg-Saint-Honoré, although he avoided hosted events and their hordes of guests. His stays grew longer and longer, but he would always return, without warning, to his shabby lodgings in Montmartre, to the waiting wife with whom he struggled to get along.[51] Then, for weeks, there would be no sign of him. Coco had to wait patiently, quiet and valiant, despite wanting so much to keep him with her and break the bonds of fate.

But his independence was the very thing that she admired in him, his ability to withdraw from society and all its charms, his singular way of mingling with artistic and literary movements without necessarily belonging to them. A supporter of Cubism, recognized as a precursor by the Surrealists, and in the vanguard of poetic thought, he nevertheless rejected all labels. Until the end of her days, Coco would read Reverdy's poems aloud and considered him one of the greats, a genius on a par with Picasso, whom she also held in lofty esteem.

She often remarked regretfully to Tiny that 'he did not have the success of Cocteau'. As Michel Leiris suggested, 'If Reverdy did not have the audience he deserved, was it not because of this fierce authenticity, which drained all brio from his work and which brought him, in his dealings with the literary milieu, to deliberately carry himself like a peasant from the Danube, or even like an Iroquois?'[52] Coco would have been more likely to borrow the words of Aragon, who said of Reverdy: 'He was, when we were twenty years old – Soupault, Breton, Éluard and I – the purest thing in the world. Our immediate elder, the model poet.'[53]

Purity: that was precisely what Coco aspired to in those dizzying days of excess. She hosted parties where artists and socialites rubbed shoulders – *Tout-Paris*, as the crowd was known – and held intimate dinners, bringing together at her home the great talents and luminaries of the age: Picasso (who for some time even had his own room), Juan Gris, Sergei Diaghilev, Jean Cocteau, Paul Morand, Igor Stravinsky, Erik Satie, Darius Milhaud, Max Jacob, the caricaturist Sem, and of course Misia and José María Sert, as well as the Count Étienne de Beaumont and his countess, who brought Coco into the most prominent of spheres. Christian Bérard, the young designer and future icon of the Roaring Twenties, would also become a regular there.

They would marvel at the harmonies of beiges and whites in the living room, that immense panelled living room that the home's mistress had outfitted to her taste, adding here and there a baroque touch from the Serts, crystals, bevelled mirrors, consoles, brown velvet curtains with gold braids, plush rugs, beige sofas, and of course the Coromandel screens, the furniture and Eastern objects tied to Boy, as well as a black piano where Stravinsky, Diaghilev and Misia took turns playing.

When it came to fashion, Coco's intuitions were confirmed: without realizing it, she had a head start on social changes. The boyish haircuts that made the head look small and neat in a cloche hat, borrowed men's clothes, straight lines, freedom and fluidness, chemise dresses, not to mention suntans and sea bathing: Coco had done it all already. Resolutely modern, she gave her dresses numbers instead of names, at a time when her competitors were still giving their designs poetic names like *Heure câline*, *La Rencontre* or *Viendra-t-il?* The Roaring Twenties belonged to Coco, they resembled her so closely, although less so the carefree frivolity. She would become a success in every way, earn a fortune while spending almost as much, play the patron, entertain artists at her home, and, amid unfathomable luxury, lead her life as she saw fit, coming and going as she pleased – nobody could make her do anything.

In the summer of 1922, the summer in which the bourgeoisie was being scandalized by *La Garçonne*, a novel by Victor Margueritte that led to his Legion of Honour medal being rescinded, Coco, at nearly forty years old, was as young as ever. By the end of that year, Coco's name was being spoken alongside those of Picasso, Cocteau (who was adored by an entire generation), and Honegger, the Swiss member of the Group of Six. After completing his one-act 'contraction' of Sophocles' *Antigone*, Cocteau commissioned Honegger to write the music, Picasso to design the sets, and Coco to provide the costumes. During the premiere on 20 December 1922, at the Théâtre de l'Atelier, the audience gawped at the simplified, stylized draped garments in coarse neutral wool, the brown wool cape thrown over the shoulders of Antigone, the blue-violet set hung with clusters of masks to represent a classical chorus, the Doric columns with broad black stripes and the guards brandishing shields with motifs inspired by Greek vases. Although Picasso and Cocteau's collaboration was not admired by all, especially not by André Breton and his friends, who held a demonstration on the night of the dress rehearsal, the costumes were unanimously praised, thus marking the beginning of a parallel career for Coco.

Several days after the premiere, she threw a Christmas Eve party at her house, which she called 'charming', perhaps because it cemented her new friendships, her sense of belonging in this new family of artists. Present were Morand, Stravinsky and the Serts, along with Cocteau and Satie, and all the members of the Group of Six (Francis Poulenc, Germaine Tailleferre, Georges Auric, Louis Durey, Darius Milhaud, and Arthur Honegger). In total, there were around thirty guests. Incidentally, it was at this time that Satie and the Group of Six performed at Le Bœuf sur le Toit, the fashionable new venue launched by Cocteau and his friends in conjunction with the club owner Louis Moysès, which had quickly become a gathering place for a Who's Who of names from the worlds of art, sport and high society. 'The stars of post-war Paris ultimately came from a frivolous world: their names were Chanel, Antoine, Cocteau, Moysès, Picasso and the surrealists.'[54]

However, if there was one adjective that did not suit Coco, it was 'frivolous'; she was wary of excess and flippancy and valued seriousness above all else. While Paris revelled in the Roaring Twenties, those years of compulsory euphoria, exhilarating lust for life, and reckless freedom, years in which jazz and speed were celebrated and idols were burnt, Coco was one of the rare few, alongside Reverdy, to foresee that the party would one day have to end, even though she never missed a chance to have fun.

Ascetic, intransigent and pure, as poets should be: that was how Coco believed Pierre Reverdy to be. But he was also fiery and passionate, his fits of temper distracting him from the path he had laid out for himself, as she witnessed on more than one occasion. She was everything to him: a friend, a lover, a diligent student. Reverdy's influence can be felt in her favourite poetry, the collections that filled her library – Rilke, Lautréamont, Verlaine, Mallarmé, Apollinaire, Aragon, Éluard, André Breton, Max Jacob and Supervielle – as well as *Les Caractères* by La Bruyère and *Maximes* by La Rochefoucauld. The influence of Reverdy can be sensed in some of the maxims penned by Gabrielle Chanel, which were published in the French edition of *Vogue* in September 1938: 'There comes a moment when you can no longer touch a work: when it is at its worst'; 'True generosity means accepting ingratitude'; 'You can only break down barriers that you yourself have built.'

With her own personal and rather modest literary tastes, Coco admired Reverdy's talent and found his poetry inspiring. She understood his work, his painful groping towards a thorny reality, 'on the earth cracked with pain'. She understood because she felt close to him, in communion with him, and that would always remain the case, even during the long years Reverdy spent in Solesmes. But if there was one thing that she would never admit to him, out of love but also from the desire not to upset him, it was that she had secretly played the role of patron, persuading publishers to disseminate his poetry. She owned his complete works in their first editions as well as many of his manuscripts, almost all of which bore dedications and were among her most prized possessions.

The manuscript of *Ardoises du toit* was inscribed with the following words:

> *Coco darling,*
> *I add a word to these words, so hard to reread*
> *Because what is written here is nothing*

If not that which could not be said
By a heart that loves you so dearly[55]

La Peau de l'homme, dated 1926, the year Reverdy withdrew to Solesmes to a house near a Benedictine abbey, bears this message:

You did not know, dear Coco, that shadow is the most beautiful frame for light. And that is why I have always felt the most tender affection for you. P[56]

Beneath the tall trees, Coco closes the manuscript of *Épaves du ciel*. She thinks of the hand of the author who penned these lines, sometimes hesitant, sometimes ardent. She can see him again in front of her, crossing out, correcting, and she remembers her disappointment the first time she saw him like this, not fired by inspiration or touched by grace, but bent over his work with the humility of a craftsman.

Perhaps inevitably, by dint of living in close quarters with a poet, everything began to seem possible, if not permissible, and Coco began to dream that she, too, could write. She had done some singing – as mentioned already – and had taken dance lessons during her time with Boy, who had encouraged her in all her pursuits. With the thirst for learning that she never lost, Coco listened to Reverdy say in his warm, powerful, inexhaustible voice – 'the most masculine voice I know,' Brassaï called it – that 'life was not surmountable without poetry'. When she thought she had grasped it – the images that spring forth, the mysterious emotions stirred by a verse or a line, the words that could be manipulated until the essential meaning was reached, the magic of imagination that made anything possible – Coco set to work, alone with a feverishly scribbled page.

She struggled on, well aware, even before Reverdy looked at her work, that she could not live up to her own standards. For months she practised, regularly showing short pieces of text to Reverdy for him to comment on and correct. But for the sake of her dignity, recognizing her own limits, she began to move away from poetry and, instead, turned towards aphorisms and maxims, trying, in one concise sentence, to capture her philosophy, her opinions, or her tastes: 'One can get used to ugliness, but never to negligence.' Or: 'Women can give it all with a smile and take it all away with a tear.' Ever humble to those close to him, Reverdy supported her in this endeavour; he himself was also in the habit of jotting down aphoristic-style notes to use later in his own works, much adjusted and corrected.

But it was mostly out of friendship, that loving friendship that could survive the most destructive of passions, that Reverdy agreed to help her. Their stormy affair lasted just four short, fitful years, on and off, and for Coco, the end was as sharp and sudden as the beginning. Because they had been friends before becoming lovers, she thought that everything would be simpler, that their earlier friendship would act as a guarantee, but what she had not foreseen was how alone she would once again feel.

In May 1926, true to himself and to his own poetic spirit, Reverdy decided to leave Paris at the age of thirty-seven and settle in Solesmes with his wife, in the shadow of the Benedictine abbey, where he would pray ardently. Coco felt a conflicting sense of turmoil and relief: turmoil in the face of this incomplete love affair, and relief because it was a demand that could not be denied; poetry had to prevail over everything else.

Coco had finally succeeded in gaining entrance into the only group that had value in her eyes: the world of artists. Friendships deepened, and collaborations occurred, particularly with Cocteau, who asked her to design costumes for *Le Train bleu*, a 'dance operetta' by the Ballets Russes, which opened on 20 June 1924 at the Théâtre des Champs-Élysées with music by Darius Milhaud and a stage curtain, *Two Women Running on the Beach*, painted by Picasso. Before the staging of his play *Antigone*, Cocteau praised Coco's talents: 'I asked her to design costumes because she is the greatest couturière of our time, and I couldn't imagine the daughters of Oedipus being badly dressed.' *Le Train bleu* was named after the luxurious train that connected Paris to the Côte d'Azur and the action was set on a fashionable beach in the 1920s; this made Coco's task easy since all she had to do was recreate, for the stage, the jersey swimwear and sportswear she had audaciously designed several years earlier.

While she felt that she belonged within this family of artists, deeply connected to them and nourished by them, she nevertheless remained humble: she always considered herself an artisan seriously engaged in her craft, without artistic talent of any kind. 'I was only there for the costumes,' she often said.

Nevertheless, she lived in the company of artists. She was there on the day Diaghilev met Serge Lifar, and sent her doctor to Raymond Radiguet, the literary prodigy who wrote *Le Diable au corps*, when his desperate lover Cocteau discovered he was dying. Coco was a friend in need, always there and always generous. When Radiguet died of typhoid in December 1923 at the age of twenty, it was Coco who paid for the funeral, which she wanted to be all in white. She also paid for Cocteau to have detox treatment in 1923 – and then again, four years later.

When it was a matter of illness or death, she would come running, moved by a genuine compassion but also by a wish to relive her own losses, as if they had remained tragically frozen in time, to perform the same actions and set the scene in the same way, filling the place with armfuls of white flowers.

Everyone respected Coco's discerning taste; everyone considered her a friend and an invaluable protector, without whom nothing would be possible. A patron of great perspicacity, she would sniff out talent, stay true to her own artistic tastes, and would not compromise her values by taking on bad projects. A woman who was powerful yet unusually discreet, she regularly fascinated those who came into her orbit. Stravinsky was the first to become passionately besotted, and then rejected, during the Garches period – an episode that caused great annoyance to Misia.

The rivalry between Coco and Misia grew just as quickly as their mutual admiration. The student seemed to be on the brink of surpassing the master, even though it was still Misia who reigned over the 1920s, Misia who listened, Misia who played the role of arbiter, who applauded, disapproved, and proclaimed her opinions, Misia who supported the Group of Six, who encouraged collaborations between Diaghilev and Stravinsky, Ravel, Milhaud, Auric, and Poulenc.

Meanwhile, Coco continued her rise. She had serious competitors, including Jean Patou, Madeleine Vionnet, Jeanne Lanvin, Edward Molyneux, Marcel Rochas and Lucien Lelong, but could revel in having dethroned Paul Poiret, whose style now seemed too sumptuous and theatrical, not practical enough for the era. Poiret, who dubbed himself 'the Magnificent', had often criticized Coco Chanel for her 'luxurious poverty', saying: 'Until recently, women were as beautiful as the prows of a ship. Now, they look like malnourished little telegraphers'. Blinded by his convictions, he underestimated the power of social change and began a long decline that led him to bankruptcy, a decline that was foreshadowed at the Paris International Exhibition of Decorative Arts in 1925, when Poiret presented his costly fantasies on the River Seine, in three barges named *Amours*, *Délices* and *Orgues*.

Conversely, 1925 saw Coco's philosophy in the ascendant. The pure linear styles presented at the International Exhibition were a testament to her influence. Black, her favourite colour, was celebrated: 'shadow as a frame for light', in the words of Reverdy. In an age of non-conformism raised to an art form, Coco launched a range of costume jewelry designed to highlight her stripped-down style: fakes that imitated the real thing surprisingly well. 'It's not the carats that matter: it's the illusion,' she proclaimed, and added: 'I find it nasty and vulgar to walk around with millions around your neck.

Jewelry is not made to make you look rich but to adorn you.' Her tastes spanned from jewelry inspired by the Medicis and the Byzantine empire to necklaces of glass beads and crosses made from Bohemian rhinestones, which she audaciously combined with real gemstones.

With her longstanding habit of employing high-society people, in 1924 she placed her jewelry atelier under the care of Count Étienne de Beaumont, a wealthy patron whose dances were among the most sumptuous in Paris. This time-honoured method was both a means to get free publicity for the house of Chanel, and a way to stay informed in the same way that Proust did; without setting a foot outside her own home.

6

THE DUKE'S
EMERALDS

La Pausa, Roquebrune-Cap-Martin, France, 1929. She places the compact back on the dressing table among countless golden pots and cut-glass bottles that her maid regularly refills with N°5, Bois des Îles and Cuir de Russie. On a piece of chamois leather, the one where she lays her jewelry at bedtime, pearl necklaces await her, carefully arranged. Above the tabletop, a three-panelled mirror reflects her image, emanating a sense of confidence, a certain allure in her golden-brown gaze.

In this moment, Boy's words come back to her: 'I often forget that you're a woman. Don't forget you're a woman.' It was a reproach, when he found her too harsh, too sharp. She softly repeats the words, but believes the advice to be outdated, even if it came from Boy. If he were still alive, she would tell him he didn't understand. She feels she has matured, able to see how far she has come. She puts on a pair of sapphire and diamond earrings, her favourites, then, one by one, the bracelets of glass beads, enough to weigh down her wrists and make her gestures emphatic. She wears very little makeup, just a light powder over her tanned complexion; women plastered in makeup horrify her. She never wears varnish on her short manicured nails: 'That would be a waste of time.'

She stands up and leaves her ensuite bathroom like an actress leaving the dressing room to walk on stage. Just like every morning, the bed has been made, the sheets changed. Hair combed and pinned, she sports one of the outfits that she loves to wear on vacation: trousers with a white canvas jacket – her 'beach pyjamas' – complemented with several strings of pearls. Conscious of the effect she will inevitably produce going down the hall, she lingers in front of the window, which looks onto century-old olive trees, and tastes the mixture of lavender and rose wafting through the air. She closes her eyes for a few moments.

When she opens them again, the olive branches seem to be bristling with silvery leaves. For some time now, Coco has no longer felt the same pleasure when staying at La Pausa, the Mediterranean villa with white walls and Roman tiles that she had recently had built high up in Roquebrune, not far from Monte Carlo and its casino, which the Duke of Westminster loved to visit. It was in Monte Carlo at Christmas in 1923 that she was first introduced to him by Vera Bate, whose real name was Sarah Arkwright, a British woman recently hired to work in public relations at Chanel and distantly related to the royal family.

In the middle of the villa, Coco installed a paved court-yard, planted with a single olive tree, which she climbed with pleasure and agility, as several photographs prove. In trousers and a striped top or in beach pyjamas, her outfit finished with strings of pearls and a large sun hat, she can be seen posing at the foot of the tree with her dog, a Great Dane named Gigot, or perched up in the branches, balancing with one foot in the air.

But the contentment of life at La Pausa was no longer enough: its beige and white decor, the couches in the vast main hall, the staircase she loved so much, based on the one in Aubazine, the guest rooms coveted by a stellar cast of visitors. No, none of it was enough. The Duke of Westminster, tired of longing for what Coco could not give him – the withheld love that she reserved for Boy and Reverdy – and tired of pushing away his own deep and non-negotiable desire to have a son and heir after only having fathered daughters, was making up his mind to expect nothing but friendship from Coco.

Their relationship lasted for six years, from 1923 to 1930, between the Duke's second divorce and his third marriage, but their friendship endured, as unwavering as all of Coco's friendships. For those six years, although the Duke was apparently infatuated, Coco felt more pampered and doted upon than 'loved' – although she could never bring herself to say the word. Undiscouraged by his two failed marriages, Bendor or Benny, as his close friends called him, was set on showering her with gifts and passionate letters. He hired several people whose job was to make sure Coco and himself were always in touch. He gave her the most sumptuous of jewelry, necklaces of pearls, diamonds, sapphires and emeralds, including a priceless necklace of thirty square emeralds set with rose-cut diamonds, which she wore in an irresistibly casual manner over simple dresses or black sweaters. After the war, she had it dismantled to transform it into brooches and bracelets that she gave as gifts to her loved ones.

Knowing Coco's passion for gardenias, her favourite flower, pure and precious (although she mainly used camelias

95

as a motif in her couture), the Duke of Westminster had the fragile blooms transported to her with the utmost care from the greenhouses of Eaton Hall. In the depths of winter, he had strawberries delivered in baskets from the greengrocer, sometimes with a more valuable gift hidden underneath, as on the day when Coco's *maître d'hôtel* found an emerald at the bottom of a crate of vegetables.

The Duke was imaginative and eccentric: nothing entertained him more than schoolboy pranks and playfulness, even in relationships. Without constant surprises, he easily grew bored. He hated to give gifts that were expected, preferring instead to present a modest umbrella or a pair of gloves as a Christmas gift or, conversely, to give sumptuous pieces of jewelry for no special occasion in particular. Tiny even recalled that, with no birthday or celebration to be marked, she herself was presented with a yellow sapphire necklace and ring, which Bendor got a friend to bring to her at the Ritz bar.[57]

To Tiny, born in 1926, the Duke was a godfather figure and accepted this role even though he hadn't been able to make it to Corbère on the day of her christening (his place was taken by Étienne Balsan). She always called him 'Uncle Benny', and that was how he signed the letters and telegrams he sent her.

A cousin of the King, a close friend of the heir to the throne (the future Duke of Windsor), and a childhood pal of Winston Churchill's, the Duke of Westminster was the richest man in England, and perhaps beyond. His wealth was so great that he could not put a precise figure on it. That fact is what most amazed Coco, much more so than the things he owned: the seven Rolls-Royces parked at Eaton Hall, the massive ancestral home, the countless properties around the world, many of which were in the London districts of Mayfair and Belgravia. 'At such levels, wealth is no longer vulgar,' observed Coco, who soon became accustomed to the chateau life that felt incomparably distant from her younger days at Royallieu. She became friends with Churchill, with whom the Duke of Westminster held hunting or fishing parties (in Mimizan, Landes or Scotland), as well as, later on, with the Duke of Windsor and his wife, formerly Wallis Simpson.

Bendor and Coco also met at La Pausa and at the chateau of Mesnil-Guillaume, not far from Lisieux, which Coco gifted to André in 1928. For his wedding two years earlier, she had bought him, on the advice of Étienne Balsan, a chateau in Corbère-Abères in the Pyrénées-Atlantiques, some eighteen miles from Pau.

A family film shot by André in 1929 in the gardens of Mesnil-Guillaume shows Coco with the Duke.[58] Smiling and relaxed, she can be seen playing with Tiny, who was then three years old. She is dressed in a skirt and a coat of dark cloth accessorized by flat shoes, a black beret adorned with a brooch, and pearl earrings, demonstrating how her style remained constant, whether relaxing with her family or posing for the greatest photographers. Bendor and Coco are then shown heading towards a car. With his svelte grey silhouette, the Duke displays a natural, unaffected elegance. 'He is elegance incarnate,' Coco said. 'He never wears anything new; he has been wearing the same jackets for twenty-five years.'

It was this sense of detachment that both attracted and inspired her. In fact, until 1931, the style of the house of Chanel bore a striking English influence: blazers with gold buttons; berets like those worn by the sailors on the *Cutty Sark*, one of the Duke's two yachts; soft tweeds brought from Scotland; chic and comfortable sweaters, cardigans and jackets inspired by the dress codes of London society. But with her usual audacity – the audacity that others soon emulated – Coco would pair a gemstone necklace with a sweater and let strings of pearls cascade over a cardigan.

In 1926, she launched what is still known as the 'little black dress'. The idea first came to her when she was out at the theatre one evening and glanced at a multicoloured flowerbed. More than ever, she turned black into the key to her success, recommending the shade as an antidote to poor taste and garish or dowdy colours.

This simple sheath of black crepe, with long, fitted sleeves and a skirt that stopped just below the knee, was 'a Ford signed Chanel', in the words of US *Vogue*. This daring comparison with the automotive industry marked the beginnings of a kind of standardization, the symbol of a new society where a single dress could please many people. Indeed, what Coco was promoting with the little black dress was the democratization of style: elegance for all.

It was also in 1926 that Cocteau, who regularly stayed at the apartment on the rue Faubourg-Saint-Honoré, commissioned 'the Black Swan', as he nicknamed Coco, to design costumes for *Orpheus*. Their bond was such that she had no difficulty bringing his vision to life, especially since the character of the angel Heurtebise, who personified 'the countless faces of Death', resonated with her deeply. She created simple costumes, almost invisible, for Orpheus and Eurydice, a pink ballgown for the young woman playing Death and, for Heurtebise, the angel disguised as a glazier who guides the hero and allows him to pass to the other side of the mirror, a set of workman's overalls in light blue.

The summer of 1929 brought more grief. After a stay at La Pausa, Coco and the Duke of Westminster, on the brink of breaking up, took a final sea cruise along the Dalmatian Coast on board the *Flying Cloud*. Misia Sert, thin and unrecognizable, went with them, still reeling from the shock of José María leaving her. He was already remarried to Roussy Mdivani, an exiled Georgian princess with cat-like eyes, who was a sculptor. The most painful part was that Misia had also been seduced by the young woman, so the absence of Sert and Roussy, who had gone travelling in Spain, felt like a double abandonment.

A telegram from Venice interrupted the cruise: 'Am sick. Come quick. Sergei.' Believing that he was about to die, Diaghilev had called his beloved Misia from his room at the Hôtel des Bains. Dressed entirely in white, she and Coco rushed to his bedside, leading Diaghilev to say with his final breath: 'They were so young, all in white. They were so white.' Black and white, those non-colours, would always be the embodiment of absolute beauty for Coco, truth without ornament.

When it came time to cover the funeral expenses, money was short, and it was once again Coco who took care of everything, thereby sparing Misia from having to pawn any of her jewelry. Alongside Serge Lifar and the writer Boris Kochno, Coco and Misia sailed with Diaghilev to the cemetery island of San Michele, on a black, flower-laden gondola. The scene was so theatrical, so perfect, that it seemed unreal and left Coco with a strangely beautiful memory.

Two months earlier, in June 1929, she had hosted another of her sumptuous dinners in honour of the Ballets Russes and of Diaghilev, one of those parties that the whole of Paris yearned to attend and which would have cost some 'two hundred thousand francs to entertain eighty people'.[59] Maurice Sachs, in charge of drawing up the guest list with Coco, said that he had been promised 'a thousand favours from people who feared they would not be invited'.[60]

By the end of the decade, however, the mood was no longer so festive. Despite the lively dancers, the jazz band, the caviar served by the ladleful, and the fireworks in the garden, there was a melancholy beauty to this evening in the Faubourg. The glitter of the twenties was slowly dimming, giving way to disenchantment, the crash of October 1929, the Great Depression, and the rise of fascism. 'Everything we knew was coming to an end. The ox, tired of clowning around, came down from the roof,' Maurice Sachs concluded,[61] referring to the name of the famous cabaret, Le Bœuf sur le Toit.

Fashion reflected this new solemnity, while growing more feminine. Dresses and skirts grew longer and more simple, free of frills, and requiring a perfect cut, while necklines dipped lower, revealing the body beneath evening gowns of flowing white satin. Coco was in tune with the times, finding huge success with her tweed and jersey suits, little afternoon dresses, sport and beach outfits, and diaphanous evening gowns in lace, organdy, tulle or chiffon, the embodiment of her slogan 'caterpillar by day, butterfly by night'.

At nearly fifty years old, she was at the peak of her career. More than ever, she was the personification of the Chanel style, as if it had been made primarily for her, fitting her body, her posture, and her way of being. Fashion magazines, led by the French and US editions of *Vogue*, captured her designs in elaborate photoshoots by the biggest photographers: Cecil Beaton, Edward Steichen, Horst P. Horst, George Hoyningen-Huene. In the early 1930s, when she employed some 2,400 people in her ateliers and had her own textile factory, America acclaimed her, and Hollywood was about to come calling.

After making her fortune with N°5, Grand Duke Dmitri was once again the one who facilitated the meeting. In the summer of 1930 in Monte Carlo, he introduced her to Sam Goldwyn, film magnate, dream factory boss, and proud survivor in an America levelled by the Depression. When he offered her one million US dollars a year to dress his stars – Gloria Swanson, Greta Garbo, Marlene Dietrich, Claudette Colbert, Ina Claire, Lili Damita – and to come twice a year to Hollywood, Coco, reflexively and not calculatingly, did not give an immediate answer, which, of course, only reinforced Goldwyn's belief that Chanel was what he needed. She was especially wary of the offer since it came from a country that was far from neutral in her eyes, the country where, in her childhood nightmares, her father had disappeared, the country that had courted and flattered her from the beginning, since the 1910s, as if in recompense. In the end, she accepted, but cautiously, after an exploratory field trip.

As a sign of the changing times, it was Misia who accompanied Coco this time and not the other way around; Misia whom Coco tried in vain to console, whom she showered with gifts and gowns. It was also Misia whose presence comforted her on that first trip to America, which Coco imagined as being 'to go and see her father'.

After a long crossing aboard the *Europa*, they arrived in New York on 4 March 1931. In her suite at the Pierre Hotel, Coco received an endless stream of journalists, who arrived one after the other. Seated sage-like amid countless bouquets of white roses, she wore one of her impeccable suits in red jersey, a beret adorned with a brooch, and several strands of pearls. America was delighted, flattered to its puritan roots, and keen to learn that elegance could be restrained without being austere, feminine with being artificial.

In front of a packed crowd of journalists, Coco at first looked 'rather bewildered', according to *The New York Times* on 5 March, as if she had only just realized the extent of her fame across the Atlantic. She got the hang of things fast, however, skilfully dodging any awkward questions, and taking care not to give definitive opinions on fashion. She explained that she was happy to respond to the invitation from Sam Goldwyn, but had no intention of making dresses during her trip, adding, with a false candour: 'I have not brought my scissors with me.'[62]

The copious superlatives in the US press were a testament to the nation's fascination with her, and Hollywood echoed the same sentiments: 'the biggest fashion brain ever known', 'one of the best-dressed women in the world', 'one of the greatest fortunes in France'.

On the railway station platform in Los Angeles, Coco and Misia, accompanied by Maurice Sachs, who had joined them in New York, were welcomed by Greta Garbo. During the reception held in Coco's honour at the Goldwyns', everybody else felt 'honoured' to converse with the couturière: George Cukor, Erich von Stroheim, Claudette Colbert, and most notably, Marlene Dietrich, who would soon become a loyal Chanel customer.

But Coco, who had not lost her common sense, did not let herself be seduced by that city 'where feelings were as fake as the sets', 'where, like at the Folies Bergère, once you've said the girls are pretty and there are feathers, you've said it all.' What she saw there – the way the stars were infantilized and forced to do what the producers said – was overwhelming, as were the criticisms and comments about her lack of 'sensational' designs. She dressed Gloria Swanson in *Tonight or Never* before deciding, shortly afterwards, to break her contract in its second year, despite each year being worth one million dollars to her.

Nonetheless, she returned home having gained great prestige from her Hollywood adventure. More than ever, America had its eyes fixed on her. This was all the more true because she had a new romance in her life with a regular at Paramount Studios, the director and designer Paul Iribe. Basque in origin and Coco's exact contemporary, he had famously worked with Paul Poiret and, in Hollywood, with

Cecil B. DeMille. When their affair began in 1931, Coco and Iribe were both nearing their fifties.

For the first time, Coco found herself with a man who was not tormented by metaphysical questions or chained to his past and who had lived, fought, and accomplished enough not to be beleaguered by lofty ambitions. She did, however, find him 'too complicated, passionate, angry, jealous', although she recognized her own inability to love simply. She recognized his devious side and vehemently disapproved of his nationalist political views. But in the end, out of weariness, she planned to marry him all the same.

She would have never considered it if her love for Pierre Reverdy had not experienced a rough patch, the last one before they cooled off and became lasting friends. During the years 1930 and 1931, the poet was often found at La Pausa and in Corbère, plagued by the most stubborn of doubts. At the château in Corbère, André Palasse filmed his two daughters, Tiny and Hélène, alongside Coco and Reverdy.[63] He also captured them about to set off on a hike: Coco is wearing walking shoes and thick stockings beneath her beige suit, and a hat adorned not with a brooch but with a ribbon. The long periods she spent kneeling and standing while working with models probably helped her to keep her surprisingly agile; she was always the first to climb a tree or suggest a long walk.

As soon as she could, she would leave Paris to rejoin her beloved nature. In André's home movies,[64] she can be seen by a lake, enjoying a pause during a hike, then sitting at a table in an inn with her family, the Palasses and the Bressons.

André and Robert Bresson, later a film director, had married two sisters, Catharina and Leidia van der Zee; André and Catharina married in 1925, Robert Bresson and Leidia in 1926. Robert was a friend of André and was fond of Corbère, where he enjoyed long walks and fishing trips. In the 1930s, Coco asked him to work with her as a photographer for her collections. She knew that he was a perfectionist who took a long time to deliver his shots, but she also knew that they would inevitably be masterpieces. Later she cherished each one of his films.

Reverdy returned home, overwhelmed by the bright light of Solesmes. They would see each other quite frequently after that, like two old friends, at La Pausa or in Paris. Coco worshipped him as she did Boy, the other man she had truly loved. She often read Pierre's poems out loud, forcing herself not to tremble:

> I leave you, I must go
> If you only love yourself
> I'm leaving you because I love you
> And I must go on walking[65]

Bravely – but for how much longer? – Coco continued her own work, pursuing the style she had built from the ground up, with all the stubbornness and dejection of the artist she refused to be. Paul Iribe was often around, claiming that he wanted to lighten her workload. He got involved in Tissus Chanel, her fabric factory, and brought in his brother, Dominique, as administrator. He was also bold enough to meddle with Parfums Chanel, criticizing the 1924 contract and Coco's 10%. He insisted that he was supporting her, helping her with this craft that was almost an artform, and that might devour her whole if he wasn't there to watch over her. She let him get on with things, too tired to argue, but she didn't actually listen to him.

To some onlookers, the 1932 exhibition named 'Bijoux de Diamants' looked like it might be a marriage proposal. From 7 to 19 November in the salons of the apartment on rue du Faubourg-Saint-Honoré, Coco displayed a collection of diamond and platinum jewelry based on gouache designs by Iribe: ribbons, feathers, comets, and stars arranged in a magical setting, sparkling on wax mannequins inside protective glass cases. This was the only *haute joaillerie* collection that Coco ever produced; her style usually favoured costume jewelry.

She asked Robert Bresson to take the five photographs for the catalogue. He carefully captured the details and the ethereal atmosphere, the delicate light and shadows, and the sense of movement in the jewels worn by the wax mannequins: a bracelet wrapping around a wrist, gemstones nestled in a tress of hair, a comet necklace looping around a neck.

The show was a huge success, and sparked fury from the jewellers of the Place Vendôme. The concept for this event, originally conceived by the Diamond Corporation of London, had been entrusted to Coco because she was the only couture designer believed capable of revitalizing the diamond and fine jewelry industry that had been crushed by the Great Depression.

Iribe was still trying to be involved in everything and dragging Coco into ventures that she would regret. Together, they revived *Le Témoin*, a magazine that had folded over twenty years earlier. Iribe, the principal illustrator of this periodical, which had once been famed for its brilliant satire, wanted to give it a nationalist agenda but Coco vigorously disapproved.

What's more, she did not want to share her power with Iribe: in fact, she was wary of him. Those closest to her gave warnings. André and Misia thought he was devious; Colette, a friend recently introduced to Coco by Misia, called him 'a demon with a voice of honey'. Nonetheless, Coco was still giving serious consideration to marrying him, perhaps because they were more similar than they appeared – she, the woman whose head ruled her heart, he with his insolent self-assurance – and because they shared the same toughness, tinged with mistrust, understanding the price of success better than anyone else.

To mark the date of their engagement, Iribe gave her a necklace of rubies, pearls, and emeralds on which he had engraved the date 'September 1934' and which she rarely took off.[66] Several months later, late in the summer of 1935, the two of them met at La Pausa, as they often did. As soon as he arrived, he went off to play tennis, with Coco watching from a distance. Suddenly she stiffened, struck by a sense of foreboding, an ominous feeling that would not go away. She ran towards Iribe. And there, right before her eyes, at the exact moment that she reached him, he collapsed, struck down by a heart attack. She bent over him, unable to comprehend. Her gaze was opaque, reflecting nothing. With the same gaze, she followed his body as they stretchered him away. He died in a nearby clinic. For a long time, she would remain a prisoner of what she had seen, as if left for dead by Paul Iribe's side.

From September 1935 onwards, she began to inject herself with a dose of Sedol, a morphine-based medication, every evening before going to sleep. 'To keep me going', she would say, closing her eyes, freed from the belief that she was dying too.

7
THE VIAL OF MORPHINE

The Hôtel Ritz, Paris, France, 1938. In white silk pyjamas, propped up by pillows, she is lost in a copy of *L'Âme de Dostoïevski*, a gift from Misia that contains a dedication from its author: 'To Madame Sert, my fairy godmother. A tribute to a faithful friendship. Dmitry Merezhkovsky.'[67] Although the book was published in 1922, Misia had only recently given it to Coco when she had complained, as she often did, of needing something to read. Since the death of her former lover Roussy from tuberculosis, Misia was suffering under the effects of morphine and despair, a shadow of herself. Her sight was failing, despite surgery in both eyes, and she was struggling to recover from a heart attack that had left her stranded between life and death for many weeks.

About twenty pages in, Coco sets the book on the nightstand, then casts a swift glance around the room, an act she immediately regrets; the smallest details start to trouble her as soon as night falls. Imaginary hands tug at the curtains, shadows dance in the mirrors. She seeks out these images, calling them ridiculous to make herself feel better. It must be time for her life-saving ritual. Or so she tells herself as she reaches for the vial and the glass syringe on the bedside table.

Her nightly routine has not changed for three years, ever since Iribe's death, which was laid on top of the many others and deprived her of sleep. With the aid of Sedol, she no longer found herself falling asleep in the early hours of the morning, exhausted after a night spent wrestling with her ghosts. The product, with its active ingredient of morphine hydrochloride, went to work quickly. She only had to wait a short moment before turning off her bedside lamp and, in the enveloping darkness, letting herself slide into slumber. This was thanks to Sedol, but not entirely. Sleeping at the hotel was comforting to her, in a room tucked between other rooms, surrounded by life, a stone's throw from the rue Cambon.

Coco often rented this suite at the Ritz during the 1920s when Stravinsky and his family were staying in her home in Garches or when she was escaping the endless parties at the rue du Faubourg-Saint-Honoré. But from 1935 onwards, she lived there permanently, with her own furniture. In the wake of the Paris riots of 1934 and, of course, the sudden death of Iribe, which had left her distraught, she decided to lead a simpler life and leave her grand home on the rue du Faubourg-Saint-Honoré. She occupied the same suite until the war began, spending her days at the rue Cambon and her nights at the Ritz.

For the rest of her life, whenever she said 'home' she would mean 31 rue Cambon, the place where she lived, worked and created; it was a place she could put down roots, after the certainties of childhood had been stolen from her.[68] In her furnished apartment inside the couture house, she made the characteristic decor more lavish every year: the lacquerwork, the mirrors, the chandeliers and crystal, the gold and gilded wood, with carved wooden consoles purchased from the Marquise Casati, false columns, antique masks, animal sculptures (usually in pairs for symmetry), a deep couch in beige suede, a coffee table covered with precious objects, gilded lions and vermeil boxes from the Duke of Westminster.

Alongside souvenirs from Venice and influences from Misia and José María Sert were symbols from her childhood. Here were the figure 5 and the double C motifs adorning a large wrought iron chandelier, combined with crystal and quartz pendants; over there were ears of wheat in a vase; elsewhere were wheat sheaves in bronze, wood and rock crystal, stars and constellations, lions in alabaster and stone. Nearby, inspired by the Aubazine boarding school, were a heavy wooden table, crucifixes, the marble bust of a priest, and a *Virgin and Child* in Burgundy limestone.

Boy's presence could be felt everywhere, with countless Coromandel screens (she owned as many as thirty-two of them), bookshelves, and furniture and objects from the East, including a panel of painted silk from Japan, a Bodhisattva head from China, wearing a lotus tiara, and a seated Buddha in lacquered wood from Japan. She kept all the books that Boy had recommended to her: some classic literature but mainly sacred texts, studies in comparative religion, and works on the occult, esotericism, alchemy, symbolism, power, intuition and reincarnation. Boy and Coco both loved to turn to books for the key to life's mysteries, seeking explanations, illumination, wisdom, and the love of God.

In this interior that resembled her so closely, with its subtle symmetries, and which she described as 'an extension of the soul', there was something deeply reassuring. When night fell, however, Coco felt too alone to sleep there peacefully. The apartment was on the second floor of the building, with a large hallway, a dining room, a small bedroom-study, and a bathroom. On the ground floor was the boutique, on the first floor were the presentation rooms where collections were shown, and on the third and fourth floors were her art studio and workshops. A magnificent staircase connected everything together like a backbone, its walls lined with mirrors, creating infinitely repeating reflections. Coco loved to sit on the stairs and watch without being seen, studying the expressions on the faces of the visitors, the customers, and the journalists when collections were showcased.

After André's divorce, his youngest daughter Hélène Palasse started sleeping in the bedroom-study. Coco, however, would never manage to do so, despite her best efforts. She later confessed to feeling 'far too scared'.[69]

In her suite at the Ritz, unlike at the rue Cambon, the childhood demons that haunted her as soon as night fell finally faded away, and her fits of sleepwalking, formerly so frequent, came to torment her no longer. She set up her Coromandel screens there, as if pitching a tent, and arranged her furniture. Tiny recalled being there and playing with a small rubber ball, which Coco had used to keep her fingers flexible. She also remembered watching in fascination as Coco got ready at her dressing table, jewelry laid out the day before on a chamois leather, often long pearl sautoirs combined with other necklaces, bracelets, buckles, earrings and rings. For a time, Coco rarely took off the ruby necklace she'd been given by Iribe, which she often wore with pearl drop earrings.

In 1935, she witnessed Elsa Schiaparelli – a name she never said aloud – move into a private mansion on this very same square, 21 place Vendôme, which also contained a boutique and a workshop. 'The Italian woman who makes dresses', Coco called her. The rivalry between these two diametrically opposed women was fierce: flamboyant Schiaparelli and timeless Coco.

The former was capable of dazzling invention and eccentricity. Since 1927, she had caused a stir with her wit and imagination, her surreal sense of creativity, her boldly unexpected colours and fabrics, including the famous 'Shocking Pink', her *trompe-l'oeil* motifs, and her hats in the shape of upside-down shoes or the stretch-knit design known as the 'Mad Cap'. Her collections were often variations on a theme: *commedia dell'arte*, butterflies, the circus.

'A dress is neither a tragedy nor a painting' was Coco's response, and undaunted, she set out to reinvent Chanel with every new collection. Unlike most of her peers, she did not mind being copied. 'It's not as if we could take out a patent for a dress!' she quipped. Since the rise of the left-wing Front Populaire in France and especially since the death of Paul Iribe, her wit had grown darker and more scathing.

In 1936, her workers went on strike, an act she saw as a betrayal, a stab in the back, a show of flagrant ingratitude. As early as 1929, well before paid holidays were made compulsory in France, she had begun sending her employees on holiday to Mimizan, on the Landes coast, where she rented a seaside villa for them, Le Pylône. (This was innovative in its day, although Jeanne Lanvin and Jean Patou also did the same thing.[70]) Now they were asking her for a raise when, Coco claimed, their pay was 'already more than reasonable'. Worse yet, they stopped her from entering her own couture house. She found herself forced to meet their demands and held onto a lasting grudge, as well as a fear, widely shared in wealthy circles, of riots and popular uprisings.

Coco had never been so transformed by tragedy and mourning as she was in those pre-war years; her beauty was at its peak, and she was more aware than ever of her own allure. She understood the power of images and the way that a portrait could become a tool. She set the scene for every picture: looking pensive in her wing chair or reclining on her beige couch, a book in hand. She was photographed by the greatest: Man Ray, Cecil Beaton, Horst P. Horst, François Kollar, Roger Schall, Boris Lipnitzki. She became the personification of her own perfume, Chanel N°5, posing in a splendid black dress in her suite at the Ritz for a 1937 advertisement in *Harper's Bazaar*. Other photographs show her on the arm of Christian Bérard, in conversation with Georges Auric and Salvador Dalí after a performance by the Ballets de Monte Carlo, or with Igor Stravinsky and Marie-Laure de Noailles after a dress rehearsal.

This was the era when her 'Maxims and Sentences' were published in *Vogue* Paris,[71] when she regularly posed with a half-smoked cigarette, and when she was rarely seen without her matt black or white enamel cuff bracelets with their detachable Maltese crosses. These iconic pieces of jewelry

THE VIAL OF MORPHINE

were made for her by Fulco di Verdura, a Sicilian aristocrat who designed some of the finest Chanel jewelry before leaving to found his own company in New York.

In 1937, she designed the costumes for her friend Jean Cocteau's production of *Oedipus Rex*, in which the young Jean Marais made his stage debut, nude beneath a flimsy binding of ribbons. Following her sure instincts, she continued to dabble in cinema. In 1938, she had a customary flash of brilliance that she turned into a costume worn by Michèle Morgan in *Quai des Brumes*: 'A raincoat and a beret, that's all. The dress is secondary.'

In 1939, her expertise was expressed to its fullest in the costumes for *La Règle du jeu*, a masterpiece by her friend Jean Renoir, son of the Impressionist painter Pierre-Auguste Renoir. Despite his bourgeois background, Jean was obsessed with social justice and supported the Front Populaire: he was moving towards the working class, while Coco had sprung from them. Their bond was a deep one, with the two of them creating a shared vision for this powerfully dark film that used costume to communicate the class differences between the characters.

A few years earlier, when Jean Renoir was making *Une partie de campagne*, Coco had recommended he hire as an assistant a young man in whom she sensed talent: Luchino Visconti. Since the 1910s, she had possessed an unsurpassed understanding of modernity, artists, pioneers; since the 1910s, she had been the embodiment of women's emancipation and had continued to fight for it. She was an equal to men – independent, rich, the head of the flourishing business that bore her name – and she was also an equal to artists. She was their friend, their confidante, sometimes their patron, and sometimes their lover too.

The list of writers, poets, composers, musicians, dancers, directors, choreographers, painters, designers, and sculptors that she considered friends cannot be reduced to just a few names, so broadly does it span the history of the 20th century. In addition to those already mentioned above, there were Salvador Dalí and Gala, Apel-les Fenosa, Colette, Francis Picabia, Georges and Joseph Kessel, and Paul Éluard. These artists were people she would never disavow, even after the war (she offered protection to Serge Lifar and Jean Cocteau during the liberation of France, for example). The list of those she helped financially is no easier to establish, as this was done with the utmost discretion, much in the way the wealthiest parents had financed the poorest pupils at the Moulins boarding school.

'My daughter has regained hope and courage. I owe it to you'; 'It's thanks to you that we are all here'; 'Thank you for the cheque', Paul Éluard wrote to her.[72]

There was evidence of profound gratitude in the letters received by Coco, letters to which she never replied; she hated writing and, especially, hated leaving traces of herself. Other letters contain declarations of love or friendship, or evidence of ongoing conversations.[73]

Jean Cocteau:

'My Coco, without you I cannot live. I love you, and if it is with true love that I love you, you mustn't hold it against me. In short, without you, without your strength, your calm, your advice, your smiles, I am just a poor lost fellow. Never leave me, that would be a crime.'

'You have no flaws, no haziness, no hesitation. You are cut from a beautiful and noble cloth.'

Pierre Reverdy:

'Dear Coco, it is marvellous how you can do me so much good with just one word, straighten me out in my desolation, in the midst of my ruins.'

'I kiss you as many times as there are letters on this paper' (at the end of a ten-page missive).

'I am sending you this foreword all the same, which I would like you to read. I didn't dare do it the other day because you know how much I hate the idea of bothering you. [...] Besides, you have so many other burdens to bear!'

'Dear, dearest Coco, if I wrote you every time I thought of you, it would be many times a day, every day that the sun rises and sets.'

Reverdy did indeed write to her constantly, sharing every detail of his life away from her, even though they met regularly in Paris or at La Pausa. He asked her to destroy his letters, and she did so, but kept a few of them to re-read in secret, as she did with Boy's notebook.[74]

The dedications written to her were no less eloquent than the letters.[75]

Paul Morand: 'To Coco Chanel, friend of lost causes.'

Jean Cocteau: 'To Coco, an admirable sister.'

Pierre Reverdy, on *Les Épaves du ciel*:

'To my very dear Coco, with my whole heart until its last beat.'

On *En Vrac*, a few year's before Reverdy's death:

'Here, dear, dear Coco, is the moment I've been waiting for, to tell you that, beyond everything, I still think of you and love you as I always have.'

In her library, Coco marked her favourite books with a simple C in pencil. Either written or recommended by friends, Coco saw these books as interconnected and forming a sort of network of comforting circularity.

Although she could only rarely get away from her business obligations in Paris, she made La Pausa available to those that she loved, and everything there was designed for their comfort: separate bedrooms, an English-style self-service buffet, a car, and permanent house staff that included a driver, a *maître d'hôtel*, a cook and her assistant, a housekeeper, and two gardeners. The account books prove that people were always welcomed there in splendid style.[76]

Dalí wrote long missives to his hostess from La Pausa, where he often stayed with Gala – and with Pierre Reverdy. He even had his own studio at the bottom of the garden. He called Coco 'his little *Capsigragne*,' an extravagant nickname that meant nothing, and started his letters with 'Dear little beautiful sweet *Capsigragne* Coco' or with 'Dear beautiful, little, and tender Coco'. In his letters from La Pausa, he often talked about his creative process, such as in this example: 'So it was necessary, my dear Coco, that all the imagination that you have, and that I had inside, that I take it out, and that I be able to paint from nature, to paint imagination from nature.'[77]

In September 1938, Coco left for La Pausa to meet the Palasses, Pierre Reverdy, Maria de Gramont, her husband

(François Hugo, goldsmith and great-grandson of Victor Hugo), their son Georges, Salvador Dalí and Gala. They were joined later by the art dealer Pierre Colle and a friend. Tiny, who was twelve years old at the time, remembered seeing them all huddled around the radio, frozen with fear, hearing the voice of Hitler talking about the Sudetenland crisis.

France entered the war nearly a year later. Dalí and Gala left Paris for Arcachon. They invited Coco to come to the large villa they had rented for six months. 'There, in any case, you will have your own room with a bathroom,' Dalí explained. 'It would do you some good to come over here and truly relax.' He finished with: 'Mostly, just come to see us soon. I send you many kisses, *Capsigragne* of my heart.'[78] The couple would eventually pass through Portugal before arriving in the USA.

When war was declared, Coco was one of the first to close her business. She did so out of patriotism and most of all because of not wanting to work for the enemy, as well as to avoid profiting from the conflict, as she had done during the Great War when she, with Boy's support, had begun her meteoric rise. In other words, she wished to 'atone' for what she now considered a wrong. Rumours ran rampant that she was stepping back because of competition from her rivals – Elsa Schiaparelli, in particular – or that she was taking petty revenge for the humiliations of 1936. But she was often the subject of jealousy and false rumours, even more so after her death.

So it was that in September 1939, just as André Palasse and his brother-in-law Robert Bresson were being enlisted,

Coco took the radical decision to close her couture house and lay off her staff. Only the boutique on the rue Cambon was kept open, to protect the entire building from being requisitioned. She announced: 'It is no longer the moment to make dresses or to style women whose husbands are going off to be killed.' Above all, she declared, 'I will not work for those people. I will not work for the enemy.'

Few couturiers responded as she did. Madeleine Vionnet also closed her couture house. Edward Molyneux sought refuge in London. Elsa Schiaparelli left for the United States in June 1940 for a series of fashion lectures, but she returned a few months later to release a collection which included, notably, jackets bedecked with fruits and vegetables to denounce Vichy food rationing.[79] She then returned to New York, where she stayed until the end of the war, although she retained her Paris couture house, which she had entrusted to an administrator. In her memoirs, Schiaparelli wrote: 'The French were working to keep themselves and their families and their country alive, thus following the oldest instinct in the world. If they had stopped everything and if the Germans had turned France into a vast cemetery, what good would that have done?'[80]

It is a fact that many couture designers continued to work during the Occupation. According to the historian Dominique Veillon, 'The grands couturiers, like other trade associations, displayed the whole gamut of attitudes towards the Germans, ranging from minimal cooperation to complete collaboration.'[81] In the majority of cases, there was a middle ground between refusal to work and collaboration: 'Between the two, the moderates held on for better days, contenting themselves with a minimum of cooperation.'[82]

Some, on the other hand, immediately began to play the game of collaboration; these included Jacques Fath, Maggy Rouff, and Marcel Rochas, all three of whom were well known to the intelligence services:[83]

'The House of Jacques Fath was frequented by a German clientele. Mrs Fath, the former model, an attractive, intriguing, and astute woman, was known for her close relationships with various German officers.'

'Maggy Rouff, a significant collaborator, received the Germans at her home, fully committed to the Boche cause. She got rich working with and for for these men.'

'Marcel Rochas, a collaborator who stood out among the rest. In 1940, his house was bailed out by the Germans. He implemented, to the letter, all the principles of the system so beloved by the Third Reich, a regime for which he did not hide his admiration. His biggest dream was to open a couture house in Berlin.'

The case of Lucien Lelong is more complex. As the president of the Chambre Syndicale de la Couture (the fashion industry's trade association) from 1936 to 1945, he tried to save French couture and the jobs it provided, and to prevent Parisian fashion from being moved to Berlin. He would be criticized for this at the end of the war: 'This involved a certain degree of compromise, which he had to justify after Liberation.'[84] (In 1941, the same Lucien Lelong hired Coco's future great rival, Christian Dior, as a designer, following Dior's early work with Robert Piguet in 1938.)

But fashion under the Occupation happened without Coco Chanel. Pierre Reverdy supported her decision; that was enough for her. He wrote her: 'Coco, dear, what a joy to receive your kind telegram. But how could I not torment myself knowing you are in Paris? [...] Yesterday, I learned that you had closed the house. I believed that would happen from day one. I wonder who was with you at that time – and I keep allowing my imagination run away with me. But most of all, darling Coco, don't stay unnecessarily exposed, and remember that those pigs will never leave Paris intact.'[85] He himself opted to stay quiet, choosing to stop writing after the publication of *Plein verre* in 1940, and refusing to publish anything in periodicals. It was, in his own words, 'a pact with silence'.

The German advance pushed Parisians out onto the streets. More than three-quarters of them tried to flee the capital. On 14 June 1940, Paris was declared an open city. On 17 June, Marshal Pétain spoke: 'It is with a heavy heart that I tell you today that the fighting is to cease.' On 22 June, the armistice was signed.

Pierre and Paul Wertheimer left France in June 1940 to seek refuge in the USA. Before they left, they had taken care to sell their shares in Parfums Chanel as well as those in the Société d'Emboutissage et de Constructions Mécaniques (SECM) and those in the firm of Bourjois to Félix Amiot. Amiot was their long-time partner, with whom they had co-founded SECM, a major name in aeronautics, on 25 July 1916.[86]

Coco also fled Paris in June 1940. Her suite at the Ritz was emptied, her furniture and trunks were brought to the rue Cambon, and her tab was paid. When the war began, in

October 1939, she had written to her two brothers to inform them she would be pausing her financial assistance: until then, Coco had always sent them a monthly allowance.[87] More than ever, her family circle tightened around André, Catharina, and their two daughters, Tiny (born Gabrielle) and Hélène.

She left for Corbère, taking with her some ten workers from the House of Chanel who had nowhere else to go, as well as Manon (the *première d'atelier*), Marie-Louise Bousquet (editor of the French edition of *Harper's Bazaar*), Dr Thérèse Boudeilles (her doctor), Angèle Aubert (her long-time right-hand woman), Aubert's husband, who had worked with Boy, and their daughter Amyt. The Bressons and Amyt's fiancé joined them later. A series of journeys were made to Pau by train or car. Coco was not short on money; she had amassed a fortune in the 1920s and 1930s. She took with her gold and jewelry and even had a Renoir painting she had purchased in 1941 sent to Switzerland.[88]

In Corbère, this little group was reunited with Catharina, Tiny and Hélène. Not far away, at the château in Auga, Étienne Balsan, his wife Suzanne, and their daughter Claude, all of whom the denizens of Corbère saw regularly, also opened their doors to family and friends. Later, they would 'hide a Jewish family in the chateau', according to Quitterie Tempé, granddaughter of Étienne Balsan.[89] This information was confirmed by the then-Mayor of Auga.[90]

On 22 June 1940, the day the armistice was signed, Coco locked herself in her room, weeping. Tiny remembered having seen her cry only twice: on that day and much later, on the death of her beloved aunt Adrienne.[91]

Acting as a wartime godmother to the actor Jean Marais, who had now enlisted, Coco took his whole company under her wing, sending them sweaters, balaclavas, gloves, and more. Marais recalled: 'she also inquired about soldiers who were married or had families, asking for their addresses and sending toys, dresses, sweaters or jewelry for Christmas, as if they were presents from their husbands or fathers.'[92] The subject of absent men – husbands or fathers – reawakened an old pain in her.

Coco had not intended to return to Paris, but when André was captured and transferred to a prison camp in Germany, she changed her mind. During a confrontation, André and a comrade named Roger Plassais had been sharing a bicycle, but André refused Roger's offer to use it to flee and ended up in the camp. (After the war, Plassais was offered a job with Tissus Chanel, as a symbol of gratitude.)

The news that he was now a prisoner came as a tremendous shock. From that moment on, Coco had only one obsession: to free André. 'I would have gone to the Devil himself, I would have died, I would have taken my own life if the worst had happened to André,' she said much later.[93] Taking her own life was no vain threat for Coco, in the wake of the suicides of her sisters, the brutal losses of Boy and Iribe, and the death of her mother from tuberculosis and thwarted love.

In July 1940, Coco returned to occupied Paris with Marie-Louise Bousquet, determined to save André. They made a stop in Toulouse, where they met up with Apel-les Fenosa, a sculptor colleague of Picasso and a friend recently introduced to her by Jean Cocteau. A few days later, they stopped in

Vichy, where Coco said she was shocked to see the champagne flowing: 'Look, it's high season!' she noted, sarcastic as ever.

Back in the capital – and not the only one, since thousands of Parisians returned to the city between July and September – she was worn down by waiting. Many of her friends had fled and were in the *zone libre* or abroad. At the rue Cambon, there was little to do except host her scattered acquaintances who had remained in Paris, just as she always had. She sang and played the piano, did her own tarot readings, deciphering only what she wanted to see, and tried to contact the spirits.

In his diary, Paul 'Boulos' Ristelhueber, former secretary to José María Sert and friend of Misia, recorded the distractions that Coco's place offered to the Serts, as well as Jean Cocteau, Serge Lifar and Paul Morand: 'Arriving at Coco's, I overhear astonishing vocal exercises. [...] Coco is listening like a good pupil [...]. She's having a singing lesson. "It's unbelievable!" Misia says to me on the way home. "At fifty-four! – And she seriously thinks that her 'voice' has a future!"'[94]

Most of all, Coco tried in vain to control her anxiety. She knew that André was in poor health, with respiratory issues that were a fearful echo of her own mother's tuberculosis. It was unbearable for Coco to imagine him in a prison camp, breaking stones, with water around his ankles, slowly wasting away, sick and weakened, choking and spitting blood. Unbearable for a mother, for it was indeed a mother's pain that she felt.

It was that moment when Baron Hans Günther von Dincklage chose to make an opportunistic appearance.

However – and let's be clear from the start – it was not he who would get André Palasse released.

She had first met Dincklage in London, where she often went (as did Dincklage, officially to see his sister). This was well before the war, late in 1934. He was married at the time, and Coco was about to marry Iribe. She remembered the year because she had been wearing the necklace Iribe had given her. To her, Dincklage had seemed 'distinguished, speaking good French, and especially English, his mother tongue'.[95]

The Baron had an English mother, Marie-Valery Kutter-Micklefield, and a German father, Georg-Jito von Dincklage. He had family across the Channel, including 'a sister in London, with whom he was in regular contact'.[96] In 1927, he had married Maximiliane von Schönebeck, whose half-sister was Sybille Bedford, the well-known writer. Because Maximiliane was Jewish, they were divorced in 1935 following the introduction of the Nuremberg Laws, but they nevertheless remained close. Her nickname was 'Catsy' and Dincklage's was 'Spatz', meaning 'sparrow' in German.

During the 1930s, Catsy and Spatz formed a duo of spies operating in North Africa and on the Côte d'Azur in southern France, most notably in Sanary-sur-Mer. French intelligence kept close watch on them; this is attested by numerous reports and notes held in the French Ministry of Defence archives, the Paris Police Prefecture, and the French National Archives. They socialized with French naval officers, and Catsy became mistress to one of them, Charles Coton.[97]

In September 1934, Dincklage was discharged from his post as press attaché at the German Embassy in Paris. Under the cover of this position, he had worked to disseminate German propaganda in France. According to notes made by the 2nd Bureau dated October 1934, 'his attitude seemed too lazy', and 'he failed to act with enough energy'.[98] In 1935, he therefore went to Switzerland to lay low.

But it did not take long for the couple to resume their work. In 1938 and 1939, they could once again be found in Algeria and Tunisia: 'Dincklage is responsible for monitoring the situation in North Africa.'[99] Catsy continued to have lovers in high places, especially in the French Navy and French National Defence. 'Baroness von Dincklage is the mistress of Pierre Gaillard, an engineer working for National Defence, in charge of a department that is both large and secret. [...] It is feared that, under her continuing influence, he may benevolently commit indiscretions likely to harm National Defence.'[100]

Dincklage, too, used his charms to recruit French women to spy on his behalf along the Côte d'Azur. But his greatest success was in surrounding himself with a throng of society ladies whose trust he had gained. Some enjoyed his charming company chastely; others became his mistresses, such as Baroness Hélène Dessoffy in 1938 or Gertrude Lowe in 1940.[101] All considered him an incorrigible seducer, an idle socialite rich enough not to have to work, a cosmopolitan aristocrat by trade.

It was precisely this ability to appear harmless and seduce society women that piqued the interest of German intelligence. None of these women were suspicious; none imagined that Dincklage could be an agent. And nor did Coco, who openly received him at the rue Cambon.

He sensed her loneliness and courted her attention, charming her friends and being able to switch effortlessly between English and French. Acknowledged as handsome man, he was tall in stature with light blue eyes. He was forty-four years old, while Coco was fifty-seven. She knew that women admired him, and that was another reason to be seen with him. He appealed to her vanity, and he also offered a distraction. There were so many reasons for Coco to accept him and invite him in, especially because she believed him more English than German.

Dincklage was so skilled that he aroused interest at the highest levels. During the 1930s, French intelligence were curious about his real duties. Notes from the 2nd Bureau recorded in 1938: 'He seems to be carrying out clandestine activity. He has likely succeeded in winning the trust of numerous French citizens. Until now, Dincklage, who is the subject of close surveillance, has yet to be caught in the act';[102] 'Former attaché of the German Embassy in Paris, he says he was dismissed by the government of the Reich. He has no profession, and the provenance of his resources is unknown.'[103]

After the war, on 7 January 1947, France's Directorate of General Intelligence concluded the following: 'Dincklage was in Paris during the Occupation, yet it was not possible to determine where he lived at the time nor the exact nature of his activities.'[104] It was also established that the Gestapo had tried to eliminate him and that he had been seen in a British military car: 'He is on the worst of terms with Otto Abetz [German Ambassador during the Occupation]'; 'The Gestapo tried in vain to liquidate Dincklage'; 'Spatz, who is said to have worked for the Germans during the Occupation, was seen in Paris in a British military car.'[105]

Perhaps most remarkable of all was that within this web of spies, cronies, double and triple agents, Dincklage also raised the interest of the Germans. Walter Schellenberg, head of German counter-intelligence, had his own doubts. During an interrogation carried out by MI6 in July 1945, he said that 'Dincklage may have had some working connection with the Abwehr but this he is unable to confirm'.[106] Questioned in 1947, Eugen Feihl, former press attaché at the German Embassy, testified to the following: 'I must say that I later suspected Mr von Dincklage of working for a counter-intelligence service, but I had no proof.'[107]

What is certain is that no one at the highest levels knew what Dincklage was really up to. What is also certain is that Coco was of interest to him: her fame, her address book, and, most of all, her ties to England and Churchill could all have made her useful.

With this in mind, years after their first meeting in London, Dincklage reappeared at an opportunistic moment: after André had been taken prisoner. And the conditions of André's imprisonment only grew worse after a visit to the rue Cambon by a German officer.

This event was recorded by Maurice Garçon, the great lawyer and future member of the Académie Française, and his testimony matches what Tiny recalls. In his journal, Garçon mentions Coco only once, on 22 October 1940:

'Lunch with Coco Chanel. She received a visit from a correct, courteous, polite, friendly German officer, charged with the mission of questioning her about her business, the number of Jews she employs, the origin of the company money. He asked about the photograph of a young man. "Who is this?" – "My nephew." – "Where is he?" – "In a prison camp. At the moment, he is employed as a farm worker. He is not too unhappy with his lot." The German did not inquire further. He came back several days later. "We want to be kind to you." – "I'm not asking for anything." – "Give me the name and the address of your nephew. We'll send him back to you." A letter from the nephew informed his aunt that they had just taken him back to the prison camp. He didn't understand what was going on.'[108]

By Tiny's account, her father had been transferred from the prison camp to a farm because he was suffering from tuberculosis. He stayed with a farming family who were living in extreme poverty. He had managed to save their only cow, which had been suffering from ruminal bloating, and had found a way to restore strength to their son, who had been reduced to eating dirt. In return, he was treated fairly well. But one day, they had come to get him and took him back to the prison camp. He hadn't understood why.[109]

Dincklage was not the only one who knew that Coco was a friend of Churchill and thought she might be useful. The Germans knew about her vulnerability and wanted to utilize it: André would be saved, but she would owe them. She did not, however, provide a single piece of information in exchange for his release.

8

STRAVINSKY'S ICON

Hotel Ritz, Paris, France, 1941. In occupied France, the Germans requisitioned a number of buildings for their troops and administrative staff, including hotels. The most luxurious were reserved primarily for senior officers and general staff. In Paris, the Ritz was assigned to the Luftwaffe (the German air force), the Hôtel Lutetia to the Abwehr (intelligence and counter-intelligence), the Hôtel Meurice to the Kommandantur (city commandant's office), and the Hôtel Majestic to the Militärbefehlshaber in Frankreich (MBF), the German military command in France.

The Ritz was only partially requisitioned. Marie-Louise Ritz (widow of the hotel's founder, César Ritz) and Hans-Franz Elmiger (manager and nephew of the majority shareholder and whom Coco always called 'Monsieur Ritz') managed to retain a section of their establishment because they were Swiss nationals. So while the wing overlooking the Place Vendôme (where Coco's suite was located before the war) was requisitioned by the Luftwaffe, the other wing, facing the rue Cambon, continued to welcome guests. The military did not use the guest entrance, and the guests did not have access to the occupied wing.

In February 1941, Marie-Louise Ritz and Hans-Franz Elmiger offered Coco a room on the rue Cambon side. It was a rather modest room on the top floor, just under the roof, with a dressing room and bathroom. Official records state that Coco had permission to stay at the Ritz as one of the 'private clients who live in the non-requisitioned portion of the hotel'.[110] To Misia, who was surprised that Coco could be satisfied with such a small room and who advised her to look for another hotel, she responded: 'What's the point? Sooner or later, the hotels will all be occupied.' (She retained the same room, which she thought rather monastic, until her death, and it was there that she breathed her last breath, on 10 January 1971.)

Throughout 1941, she continued to spend her days at the rue Cambon and her nights at the Ritz, where she stayed until late morning. On her new bedside table, next to the book she was always reading, she placed the icon painting that Stravinsky had given to her. She never parted with it and asked for it to be buried with her, along with the little yellow ring given to her so many years before by the Roma woman in Moulins. Tiny ensured that this wish was granted.[111]

In her grief, hoping in vain for André's release, she felt supported by the two men she truly loved: by Boy, from the world of the spirits, and by Pierre Reverdy, the poet now in Solesmes. She read and re-read Boy's notebook in secret, and recited Reverdy's poems aloud like prayers. She struggled with dark thoughts, often speaking the words: 'I would go to the Devil himself, I would die, I would take my own life if the worst happened to André.'

One morning in March 1941, the Devil himself did appear, in the form of Baron Louis Piscatory de Vaufreland.

Just as she was leaving the Ritz to return to her 'home' on the rue Cambon, she ran into two familiar faces, Count Gabriel de la Rochefoucauld and his wife, deep in conversation with a young man: Louis de Vaufreland. To Coco's ears, the name had a pleasing ring: she had met a Vaufreland in Pau in the 1900s, a perfect gentleman from an excellent family who had been a lover of horses and a friend of Étienne Balsan.

Louis de Vaufreland, elegantly dressed and perfumed, was twenty-nine years old, of medium height with pale blue eyes and a rosy complexion, with fine red-blond hair over a high forehead. He was lively and talkative, with a tic in his left shoulder, which he would twitch as if to punctuate his sentences. He was the son of Baron Georges Piscatory de Vaufreland and Carmen Kenens, who had died twenty years earlier. He had gone to school in Paris, in the 7th *arrondissement* and then in the 16th, at Janson-de-Sailly. He had then attended at the Sainte-Geneviève school in Versailles and prepared for the Saint-Cyr military school entrance exam. After his application was unsuccessful, he had gone to study at Cambridge. Blessed with a prodigious memory and having travelled all over Europe, where he had family, he could speak five languages.[112] 'He struck me a frivolous young man, saying whatever came into his mind,' Coco said after the Baron's arrest.[113]

Right from the start, he told her that he had a way to free André Palasse, by claiming that he was vital to the running of Tissus Chanel. She listened to him and did not refuse his help, even though she had declined the offer of help from the German officer who visited the rue Cambon on 22 October 1940: 'Without me asking him anything, he spoke to me about André. He said he could bring him back. I accepted his offer on the spot.'[114]

Alas, this Vaufreland turned out to be very different from the other Vaufreland she had known in her younger days. He did get André released, but he caused great harm to Coco in return. Reverdy saw through him and went to arrest him himself after Liberation.

French intelligence reports described Vaufreland as the 'inglorious offspring' of a family connected to the great houses of France, Spain and England, 'an international idler', who, after his studies, 'lived without a well-defined occupation'.[115] He was a cosmopolitan man of many faces, fitting easily into all social circles: 'His eccentricity is an affect. Many believed him to be a fickle, frivolous and snobbish boy, incapable of real wrongdoing. Those who knew him better would say he was quite the opposite: poised, thoughtful, intelligent.'[116]

Accustomed to spending lavishly, especially in the bars where he spent the majority of his time, living off the family fortune, Vaufreland lost considerable sums in 1936 in risky London investments. Then in 1938, he went through an expensive divorce. This angered his father, who began to send him an allowance too modest to support his usual lifestyle.[117] The young man was in constant debt and short of money, but nevertheless continued to 'live in a very grand style'.[118]

He therefore began to gravitate towards those who had the most to offer: 'Profoundly amoral, he commits treason for money.'[119] Versatile and opportunistic, he was pro-French and British one day, pro-German the next, and pro-French and British the day after that. 'He seems to be playing the role of double agent, with regard to the British and French authorities as well as the German ones,'[120] said a confidential note from the Vichy Ministry of the Interior dated 10 February 1941. From London, Captain Vaudreuil, head of General de Gaulle's personal staff, wrote on 21 May 1943: 'Vaufreland is believed to be a spy in the pay of Germany, although he has recently sought to secure payment from the Allies.'[121]

On 22 March 1941, Vaufreland was recruited by Hermann Niebuhr, lieutenant in the Abwehr, section III F (the section devoted to counter-intelligence), and by Sonderführer Albert Nottermann. He immediately told them that Coco Chanel, with her English ties, might be of interest to them. He claimed that she was 'his cousin', but of course this was just another lie.[122]

Hermann Niebuhr and Albert Nottermann seemed happy enough to have André released, but they took the opportunity to have Coco, without her knowledge, registered as a potential agent because of her address book and her friendships with the British. She was assigned the number F.7124 and a telling pseudonym – 'Westminster', sometimes spelt 'Wesminster'. In fact, as he later confirmed to the French Directorate of Territorial Surveillance on 23 February 1946, Niebuhr 'told his superiors about the potential of this lady who could approach Churchill, the Duke of Westminster, the Duchess of York, and other British figures'.[123]

But this is not all. Niebuhr, who like Vaufreland was always short on money, had a reputation for perpetuating dubious registrations: 'The Chanel case serves as proof of this: Niebuhr had a tendency, whether for payment or to exaggerate the value of his services, to register agents with very little basis. Accordingly, Miss Chanel is listed as "F.7124 Wesminster". Yet the information stops there: no established file or report for F.7124 can be located.'[124]

Coco was, therefore, 'registered' as a potential agent, both for a finder's fee and because of her ties to Churchill. According to standard procedure, two records would be kept: a French one (kept in the archives of the Paris Police Prefecture[125]) and a German one (held at the French Ministry of Defence archives and declassified in March 2016[126]). Of course, no such file or report ever existed, because Coco did not work as an agent and provided no information. In other words, she was not in the service of the Nazis.

The promise of André's release nevertheless implies a quid pro quo. Coco wanted to give money to Vaufreland, which he refused, so instead she invited him to stay at La Pausa whenever he wished and also offered to buy him expensive furniture for the apartment he was having renovated. She begged him to accept, and he eventually did so.

But that was not enough, and in August 1941, she agreed to accompany Vaufreland to Madrid, where the warring sides and their emissaries could meet. On 5 August, they took a train with all the necessary papers.[127] The evening the two spent in the Spanish capital, with the diplomat Brian Wallace and his wife, is well recorded. Coco who simply called herself a friend of Winston Churchill, claimed that she would have preferred to be in England and threw around some platitudes about France being in a state of shock due to the Occupation.[128] This chatter did nothing to settle her debts. André's release, if it was to happen, would demand a price.

Coco did not understand any of this and had no idea (but then again, who could have?) that since the Nazi invasion of the Soviet Union in June 1941, the Abwehr, an exclusively military organization, had their sights increasingly set on preventing a rapprochement between the Russians and the British, and were therefore attempting to rouse the hostility of the British ruling classes towards Stalin.

Finally freed, André was repatriated on 11 November. He quickly learned, from Coco herself, that it was to her that he owed his salvation.[129] He could barely stand to meet her gaze. He feared being the source of serious trouble in the very near future. But should Coco have left him to die in a prison camp? What mother would be capable of the horrific (or heroic, depending on one's point of view) act of refusing the help of the enemy in order to save her son? When she accepted this, she was surely acting as a mother; she could not let the matter drop. Especially since she held firm and refused to get involved in Vaufreland's manoeuvres in exchange for André's release.

Now André was finally free, but Coco lived in fear of what they might yet ask of her. She began to lead a very secluded life, her hopes withered away. And of course, she was not working: her couture house remained closed. In stark contrast, other Parisian couturiers showed their collections to the wives and mistresses of the German officers. She did not.

After his long months in captivity, André was no longer the same. In the years after the war, he blamed Coco for her excessive love for him. He also divorced Catharina. Supposedly, he had been released so he could return to his position as director of Tissus Chanel, but he was not strong enough to work. In any case, the fabric factory, like the couture house, had been closed since September 1939.

The situation was different for Parfums Chanel, which remained in business. When André was released on 11 November 1941, it had been two months since the company had been saved, having narrowly escaped the grip of the Groupe Allemand des Alcools. The process of 'Aryanization' took seven months, from 31 January to 1 September 1941, a period that saw a fierce battle between Félix Amiot and the Germans.

According to the odious terminology of the Nazi regime, and to use the definition from the French National Archives, 'economic Aryanization' was a process designed to eliminate 'all Jewish influence in the national economy'.[130] The process was organized by the Commissariat-General for Jewish Affairs (CGQJ). According to its importance to the economy, 'property belonging to Jews was destined to be either liquidated or sold to Aryans'.[131]

As previously mentioned, before emigrating to the USA in June 1940, the Wertheimer brothers – who were Jewish – had sold the firm of Bourjois and their shares in Parfums Chanel and SECM to their partner Amiot. As businesses, Bourjois and Parfums Chanel were particularly coveted properties. The occupying authorities repeatedly claimed that the sale had been a sale of convenience and therefore a case of 'false Aryanization'. Amiot was aware of this and later declared: 'The attention of the Groupe Allemand des Alcools was drawn to the Bourjois-Chanel affair and to me, given my well-known friendship with the Wertheimer brothers.'[132]

Parfums Chanel was the only one of these businesses that involved Coco, because she was a shareholder, but she played no part in the process of Aryanization, according to the analysis of Lucile Chartain, head of the AJ/38 collection at the French National Archives: 'Coco Chanel was not involved in the Aryanization of Parfums Chanel and is only mentioned in passing in the AJ/38 file kept in the archives of the Service du Contrôle des Administrateurs Provisoires [SCAP, the Department for Oversight of Interim Adminstrators]. Its four hundred pages are mostly technical discussions between Félix Amiot, the Commissariat-General for Jewish Affairs, the SCAP, and the Paris Police Prefecture. Only two pages mention Coco Chanel.'[133]

The Aryanization process began on 31 January 1941, with an investigation request from the SCAP: 'Due to Mr Amiot's prior collaboration with the Wertheimers, the company must be considered as being under Jewish influence.'[134] Amiot was therefore forced to demonstrate that he was 'the primary shareholder for Parfums Chanel from 30 April 1940, the date on which the shares were given to him by the Wertheimers in repayment for a loan.'[135] But he found it difficult to supply evidence.

Next, as was customary, an interim administrator (who would be closely monitored) was appointed by the Germans.[136] Georges Madoux, who already held a key position at Tissus Chanel and Parfums Chanel, was named as administrator on 12 March 1941. As Madoux was slow to submit his report,[137] Amiot was eventually able to provide the documentation that the SCAP had requested,[138] which specifically attested to the fact that he was Aryan and that the Wertheimers genuinely had owed him a debt, which was connected with SECM. As evidence, he provided a telegram from the Wertheimers, which he also submitted as evidence his ownership of Bourjois. However, 'this was, for the Germans, motivation for a fast and thorough investigation; it arrived from New York and startled them.'[139] Further explanations ensued, involving Parfums Chanel, Bourjois and SECM, and forcing Amiot to fight battles on all fronts.

The German authorities continued to believe it had been a sale of convenience. Madoux had no room for manoeuvre; he was being watched closely and could provide no evidence. In his report of 10 April 1941, he therefore concluded that '520 shares still belong to Jews.' In the same document, he mentions having been 'presented with a purchase proposal from an Aryan company,'[140] which Amiot named on several occasions as the Groupe Allemand des Alcools.[141]

After months of fierce argument between the occupying authorities and Amiot, the Aryanization process seemed unlikely to be approved, which would have led to Parfums Chanel falling into enemy hands. On 5 May 1941, therefore, Coco volunteered, via a typed letter with no signature, to buy back some shares. Madoux took some time to pass this on, so much that the SCAP 'was surprised that the 5 May proposal [had], to date, not been the subject of any communication'.[142] Later, a second letter, also typed and unsigned, dated 20 June, was sent by Madoux, this time specifying the number of shares to be bought back: '520 shares that are still owned by Jews'. In other words, these were the shares that posed a problem. 'These letters were not shocking in themselves, given the vocabulary of the time,' states Monique Leblois-Péchon, former director of the AJ/38 collection at the French National Archives. 'Given the doubts about the transfer of shares, Coco Chanel and Madoux were justifiably worried about the fate of the company. Without approval, the company could have been sold to anyone.'[143]

The 20 June letter was not required: Amiot finally succeeded in gathering all necessary evidence of the sale. Consequently, Parfums Chanel no longer needed an interrim administrator, so Madoux was relieved of his duties on 26 August 1941,[144] and on 1 September 1941, 'Aryanization was deemed complete'.[145]

Parfums Chanel was saved, but for Bourjois and SECM, the battle was still not decided.[146] In 1942, the anti-Semitic collaborationist press raged against Amiot; he was subjected to a barrage of attacks from *Au Pilori* and *L'Appel*.[147] Amiot was questioned several times by the Gestapo. Fearing for his life, he sent his daughter to Switzerland. In the midst of the Occupation, he took great risks, undoubtedly to safeguard the interests of the Wertheimers, but also to prevent the deportation of workers and offer shelter to dissenters. Regardless, he still pulled in a huge profit, especially when SECM partnered with Junkers to construct 370 aircraft. He was criticized for this huge discrepancy after the liberation of France.[148]

Coco, however, had nothing to do with any of this business with Bourjois or SECM. Parfums Chanel, which bore her name, had been saved. This was a relief. After the war, it would be time to review the 1924 agreements, with which she had been dissatisfied since the 1930s. The Wertheimers knew this; they had often spoken about it together. This was especially true of Pierre, with whom Coco had always maintained a friendly relationship. In 1946, she and Tiny visited him and his family at his home in New York. In the meantime, however, she was not finished with the Germans: she still had a debt to settle.

9

BOY'S NOTEBOOK

Rue Cambon, Paris, France, 1942. The curtains are drawn in broad daylight. The whole building stands silent. Coco, who does not like feeling sorry for herself, is doing nothing, embracing her own idleness, given her decision not to work. Spread out on her beige suede couch, where, before the war, she embarked on 'her finest journeys', she opens 'Boy's notebook', as she calls it. She shows it to no one and considers it one of her most precious possessions. In the twilight of her life, while putting her papers in order, she will entrust it to Tiny, telling her simply: 'It comes to me from Boy.' In the back of the boutique on the rue Cambon, in a dark and windowless room whose doorway was hidden behind screens, she also keeps two pieces of Chinese furniture that he gave to her: a throne base and a wedding cabinet.[149]

Boy copied out passages of text into this precious notebook, sometimes in English, sometimes in French, attesting to his fascination with the East, esotericism, the history of faith and tradition, Hinduism, the great sacred texts, reincarnation.[150] There are passages from the Upanishads and the Bhagavad Gita, from *Glimpses of Unfamiliar Japan* by Lafcadio Hearn, from *Letters from a Living Dead Man* by Elsa Barker, from *Hereafter* by Isabel Butchart, from *Demi-Gods* by James Stephens.

The notebook, inscribed with the date 'January 27, 1915', opens with a preamble in English, a warning from Boy: 'It is pleasant to forget oneself in following the imagination of another, but better still to think out things oneself.' It ends with five reading recommendations, again in English: a biography of Darwinist and philanthropist John Lubbock, plus Lubbock's list of the hundred best books; a book on Freemasonry (which one is not specified); *Gleanings in Buddha-Fields* by Lafcadio Hearn; and, finally, the works of the scholar and occultist Agrippa. In other words, these were suggestions that led to other books, then on to even more, creating a spiralling sense of dizziness.

Coco used to open this notebook in her most desperate moments; it was her refuge. She would lose herself in the text, but mostly in Boy's handwriting. Her eyes remained dry, as usual, but she could easily have cried.

André was also sitting idle, and his health remained fragile. He was thinking, however, of reopening the fabric factory in Maretz, in northern France, with Gilbert Lasson, the former director, who was back from imprisonment. The factory, pillaged and occupied, had been seriously damaged early in the war. The two of them talked about the idea to Coco, who did not object. So the matter was settled: André had been released on the promise that he would run Tissus Chanel as he had done before the war, splitting his time between Maretz and Lyon (Tissus Chanel would subsequently be renamed Tissus Palasse). In 1943, the Maretz factory restarted production. Coco hoped that her debt was now paid, but she doubted it.

Vaufreland was no longer around. As for Dincklage, he began to show a different side of himself. A certain chill set in between them. After the war, he contemptuously called Coco 'the Old Lady'; after the war, they saw each other a little in Switzerland, and then not at all. She no longer considered him an idle socialite; she even believed he was a double agent for the British.

In fact, late in 1943 he came to her with an extravagant proposition: to play a part in peace talks with the British. The idea came from Walter Schieber,[151] who was 'big in artificial textiles in Germany',[152] and Theodor Momm, a friend of Dincklage, who had spent his childhood in Belgium, where his family were in the fabric trade, and who was now monitoring the French textile industry.

Coco's only task would be to write a letter to Winston Churchill to begin a dialogue. She found the idea appealing, since it would allow her to settle her debt in the noblest of ways: working towards peace on the side of the British, as she always had been.

With a combination of naivety and megalomania, she was delighted by the thought of being part of a separate peace process in the West between adversaries who no longer believed in the power of weapons. Many years later, she bragged about this to those close to her and even to her assistant, Lilou Marquand: 'Mademoiselle considered it regrettable that those in power did not consult her. During the war, she even had the idea of getting Churchill to sign a peace treaty.'[153]

Coco boldly dared to set one condition: the release of a British friend of hers, Vera Lombardi. Coco never left her friends behind and never would as long as she lived. Vera Arkwright, who had become Vera Bate and then Vera

Lombardi, had been behind her first meeting with the Duke of Westminster and Winston Churchill. She was the one who had introduced Coco to the upper echelons of British aristocracy. Now she was detained in a prison in Rome, suspected of being a spy in the pay of the British.

The ties between the two women had been firm for many years. Vera had even been hired to work at the rue Cambon, where she held an international public relations position. But they had fallen out with each other in 1937 when Coco tried to interfere in her friend's private life, as she often ended up doing with those close to her. 'She chased me away,' Vera declared to Churchill.

It must be said that Coco was, indeed, disapproving of Vera's choices. In 1929, she divorced her first husband, Fred Bate, an American officer she had met in Paris during the Great War, and in the same year, married another officer, Alberto Lombardi, an Italian and member of the Fascist Party. Although Vera and Coco had been on bad terms for several years, getting Vera extricated from her jail in Rome was a matter of duty for Coco, since she had the means to do it.

Nor was Coco acting out of her own interests: she knew Churchill well enough to take part in these vague plans for peace without Vera's help. Since the 1920s, and the fishing and hunting parties at the Duke of Westminster's home, Coco and Churchill had not lost touch. Winston had been charmed by Coco's personality from the very start. On 27 January 1927, he wrote to his wife: 'The famous Chanel turned up and I took great fancy to her – a most capable and agreeable woman – much the strongest personality Benny [Westminster] has yet been up against. She hunted vigorously all day, motored to Paris after dinner, and today is engaged in passing and improving dresses on endless streams of mannequins. All together 200 models have to be settled in almost three weeks. She does it all with her own fingers, pinning, cutting, looping. Some have to be altered ten times.' During his visits to Paris, Churchill never missed a chance to pay her a visit, sometimes lingering at the rue Cambon for dinner and wine. These meetings even took place in the early years of the war.

In late 1943, Vera's fate was decided in Berlin, as Walter Schellenberg, then head of German counter-intelligence, explained during his interrogation by MI6 in July 1945. '1. A certain Frau Lombardi, a former British subject of good family then married to an Italian, should be released from internment in Italy and sent to Madrid as an intermediary. [...] 2. Lombardi's task would be to hand over a letter written by Chanel to the British Embassy officials in Madrid for onward transmission to Churchill. 3. Dincklage was to act as link between Lombardi in Madrid, Chanel in Paris, and Schellenberg in Berlin.'[154]

Coco preferred to go to Madrid herself to discuss matters with Vera directly before writing to Churchill. Unfortunately, Vera rushed to the British Embassy to make the claim that Coco was not an intermediary but an agent in the service of the Germans.

Coco could hardly believe that Vera, whom she considered a friend despite their falling out, was capable of betraying her so viciously. The irony was that Vera was also suspected of being a Nazi agent. Once again, Coco tried to help her by writing to Churchill. This letter, written on the stationery of the Ritz

Hotel on the Paseo del Prado in Madrid, began in English and continued in French (from 'Ultimately, Vera wants to return'):

> My dear Winston – Excuse me to come and ask a favour from you in such moments as these. My excuse must be that it is not for myself. I had heard for some time that Vera Lombardi was not very happily treated in Italy on account of her being English and married with an Italian officer... You know me well enough to understand that I did everything in my power to pull her out of this situation, which had indeed become as tragic as the Fascists had simply locked her up in prison! ...I was obliged to address myself to someone rather important to get her freed and to be allowed to bring her down here with me. The fact that I managed to succeed in this has placed her in a difficult situation as her passport which is Italian has been vised [sic] by the Germans and I understand quite well that it looks a bit suspect. But as you can well imagine, my dear, after 4 years of occupation in France it has been my lot to encounter many kinds of people! How I would have pleasure to talk over all these things with you! Ultimately, Vera wants to return to Italy, where her husband is. I believe that a word from you would smooth out all the difficulties, and I could go back to France in peace, for I do not want to abandon her here. I hope your health has improved. I would not dare ask for a response from you, but, of course, a word from you would be greatly reassuring as we await the end. I remain always affectionately.

The handwritten letter is signed 'Coco' on one line, 'Chanel' on the line below, and ends with a postscript in French: 'Perhaps Randolph [Churchill's son] can give me some news about you.'[155]

The peace plan failed before it could even get started. This extraordinary endeavour-turned-fiasco was analysed years later by Sir Stuart Hampshire, a former MI6 agent and one of Schellenberg's interrogators in July 1945: 'This man had long been convinced that Germany was going to lose the war, and he favoured a separate peace in the West. But he didn't understand much about Britain or France, or about the circles in which Winston Churchill moved. His degree of ignorance surprised me during questioning. He was promoted quickly, but he was neither brilliant nor very intelligent. As for the attempt to approach the British government through Coco Chanel, it was downright grotesque. If Schellenberg had wanted to enter into negotiations with the British, he would have needed a better, more serious intermediary than her. It was naive of him to use her; she had no political value. Simply knowing Churchill was not enough to mount an operation. Schellenberg believed that Chanel, because of her friends in high society and the art world, as well as her address book, had more political power than she actually did. All of this was worryingly naive.'[156]

Since the peace plan had failed in its infancy and Coco's letter to Churchill had only been about Vera Lombardi and not a peace treaty, the form that recorded Coco's registration as a potential agent, the one that had been set up without her knowledge, was sent to Berlin on 1 June 1944. Two handwritten lines indicate that she had been 'unregistered'.[157] Her registration had been thoroughly useless.

'On 27 August 1944, Vaufreland was stopped by Reverdy the poet who, it seems, had a personal grudge against him.' So said the presentation of the Vaufreland affair that was given before the Court of Justice of the Department of the Seine on 29 March 1949.[158] Pierre Reverdy and André Palasse shared a hatred for this man who had so greatly harmed Coco. Also in August, two members of the French Forces of the Interior came looking for Coco in her room at the Ritz at 8.30 in the morning. She returned to the rue Cambon several hours later.

Contrary to what some said after her death, Coco does not appear on the 'official blacklist' drawn up by the French Forces of the Interior, a file of the Ministry of War, FFI Directorate, at the French National Archives. It is the name 'Chemel' that is registered there, not 'Chanel' (the same file records that it refers to one Marcel Chemel). Paul Morand, Jean Cocteau, and Serge Lifar do, however, appear on this list of collaborators.[159]

While the liberation of France was taking place, Malcolm Muggeridge, an MI6 agent, dined at the rue Cambon with Coco and one of her friends. In his memoirs, *Chronicles of Wasted Time*, his description of that evening was: 'really there was nothing to say'.[160] What's more, he wrote no additional reports or notes at that time, a fact confirmed by the Malcolm Muggeridge Society.[161]

Félix Amiot was arrested in September 1944. The press went crazy: 'The list of known names is starting to be whittled down.' 'Five manufacturers arrested.' Often cited among the 'collaborators', Amiot knew he risked being condemned when France was liberated because of his contracts with the Germans, but nothing came of this. After the war, he returned ownership of the firm of Bourjois, the shares in SECM, and the shares in Parfums Chanel to the Wertheimers. The only remaining source of dispute remained the distribution of SECM shares, which was not settled until the early 1950s.[162]

Coco herself was not found guilty in the eyes of French justice either. On 4 June 1948, she spoke to the magistrate Roger Serre as a simple witness in the Vaufreland affair. André Palasse did the same. The judge, who had all the documentation in hand, including those showing proof of Coco's trip to Madrid and her registration as a potential agent, considered the charges insufficient. When she learned she had been registered without her knowledge, she exclaimed: 'I protest such nonsense!' As a simple witness and not a defendant, there was no case to be filed against her: her name was simply crossed out.[163] 'This means that during the investigation, even before the verdict, she was no longer among the people being prosecuted,' explained Pascal Raimbault, curator at the French National Archives.[164] (Vaufreland, of course, was charged and sentenced.)

A year earlier, the statement by Albert Nottermann, who had, along with Niebuhr, recruited Vaufreland in 1941, had already shown Coco to be innocent. An archive file dated 30 July 1947, and classified as secret,[165] reveals that Nottermann testified during an interrogation by the Directorate of Territorial Surveillance (DST): 'I facilitated her demands for passes and released her nephew, a prisoner of war who was the director of a silk factory in Lyon. Chasnel [*sic*] never provided a single piece of information. I had her registered as an agent to justify these interventions.'

In another document, the minutes of his questioning by the DST on the subject of Coco Chanel, also classified and dated 27 September 1947, Nottermann gave more details: 'Her nephew being held prisoner in Germany, she wanted him to be released so that he could take over the running of her factory in Lyon. I intervened with the officer in charge of prisoners of war and he was released. If I rendered these services to Ms Chasnel, it was solely out of sympathy, but I asked for absolutely nothing in return.'[166]

Coco died without ever knowing that these documents existed. Classified archives bearing the 'top secret' stamp are not accessible until fifty, seventy-five, or even a hundred years after the events in question. In the case of the two documents just mentioned, the period was seventy-five years.[167]

The puzzle, therefore, can be solved by looking at the archives in their entirety. Coco gave a simple witness testimony in the Vaufreland trial; she was not on the Resistance's blacklist; she did not know she was ever registered by the Nazis as a potential agent, and that registration was never put to use; and finally, she provided no information in exchange for André's release.

Long after her death, Coco remained the victim of preposterous theories and rumours. Most were motivated by a desire to sensationalize, others by jealousy, resentment or disillusion. 'Impotence, the power of others. Not even death can protect us,' wrote Henri Michaux.[168]

10
THE DRESSMAKING SCISSORS

Lausanne, Switzerland, 1945. The mountains fade into the mist; later in the day, they will reappear, dark blue streaks floating above Lake Geneva. Coco squints but can barely make out the horizon. She sees herself as a child again, crouching in the little cemetery, gazing at the colours of Chignore above the low-built wall. From her second-floor balcony, on the white facade of the Hôtel Beau-Rivage, she savours the luxury of tranquillity. 'Luxury, it's what the soul needs,' she likes to say.

A soothing drowsiness washes over her. A land of curves and peaks, of verdant expanses and blue-tinged transparency, Switzerland is like a memory of childhood, a child's stroll to school. Comforted, Coco decides that when the day comes, it is in this land, this quiet land, that she will be buried. In Lausanne, preferably.

As she thinks back on the little girl she once was, tears nearly come to her eyes, as she stands on the balcony, away from prying eyes. On principle, however, she forbids herself from crying. Instead, she gets up, pushes open one of her suite's French doors, passes through the harmonious beiges of the living room, which adjoins the bedroom, and sits down at her dressing table. On her bedside table, she has placed the ever-present icon painting from Stravinsky, several books, and a pair of scissors made by the firm of Nogent (fine enough to cut fabric), which she takes with her everywhere. She no longer uses the scissors that she left behind in Paris, hanging from a white ribbon.

That evening, in the baroque salons of the Beau-Rivage, she joins the other famous guests: some exiles, some crowned heads from Europe or elsewhere, some simply wealthy social-ites on vacation. Wearing a chiffon gown and laden with pearls, Coco, dreamy soul that she is, dines with her friends amid the elegant hum. But at night, her demons return, and her sleepwalking becomes frequent again. She sometimes wakes to find herself brandishing the scissors, 'as if wanting to cut an invisible thread to the past'.[169]

During this long period of idleness – which lasts until 1953 – she continues to be haunted by her ghosts, by the shadows and traces of her relatively distant past: Jeanne, her mother, her sisters Julia-Berthe and Antoinette, Boy and Iribe. Now at last she allows herself to dwell on their brief lives, allows herself to listen to them. Her war-time acquaintances, whether by choice or obligation, also haunt her. Dincklage, that two-timing, murky character with his ever-mysterious pursuits, the traveller that Coco should never have tried to detain. Vaufreland, Momm and Schellenberg, those passing shadows, those ferrymen between one world and another, from the world of the living to the chilling world of horror and lawlessness.

Shifting and contradictory feelings swirl over her. First, a sense of injustice, given that she had closed the house of Chanel at the start of the war and stood firm against the

Germans after André's release. Then, a feeling of remorse, of piercing guilt, tumbling around inside her, the vague sense she had done a deal with the devil to save André. She did not talk about it, of course, and contented herself with railing against France, which did not love her, which had never loved her, while America supported her through everything, a perennial source of comfort.

In the winter of 1945–46 in Saint-Moritz, she was reunited with Paul Morand and his wife. Morand, who had taken an oath of loyalty to Marshal Pétain, had been expelled from the diplomatic corps in September 1944. He subsequently 'retreated' abroad. Many years later, these conversations between these two bitter souls, back together in a golden Swiss palace, would be turned into *The Allure of Chanel*, published in 1976. In that book, Coco confides: 'In any case, I shall never rest during my lifetime. Nowhere would I worry as much, or exhaust myself as much, as in a rest home. I am well aware how bored I would get in heaven, even on an aeroplane I get more bored than I do on the ground.'[170]

When she left Paris shortly after the liberation of France, it was partly to get away for a while from what she called 'the grim atmosphere and the settling of scores'. But primarily it was once again to help André, who was being treated for tuberculosis in a Swiss sanatorium. As usual, Coco took care of everything, renting him an apartment and later a house. He never returned to work again.

But until 1953 and her return to the world of Paris haute couture, Coco regularly travelled back and forth from the French capital. There she went back to her little room at the Ritz and her apartment where Hélène Palasse, Tiny's sister, was living temporarily. During that period, her other destinations included La Pausa, the French spa town of Dax for treatments in 1947 and 1948,[171] Venice, Sestriere, London and New York.

During these post-war years, she often saw her friend Maggie van Zuylen in Switzerland, Paris, New York or the Netherlands, where the van Zuylens owned a chateau. From a modest family, Maggie had been born in Alexandria as Marguerite Namétalla. She had hypnotic green eyes and a sharp wit, and had married Baron Egmont van Zuylen. Although she was Jewish, it was she who gifted Coco the Egyptian locket engraved with one of the 'Throne Verses' from the Quran, believed to have protective properties. Tiny said: 'If you gave her a gift modest in appearance but strong in spiritual and symbolic significance, you knew Coco well.' Coco never took off this locket, wearing it on the end of a long chain, tucked into a pocket of her suit.

In 1946, Coco and Tiny set off for the USA on board the *Queen Mary* for a voyage of several weeks. She had plans to see several friends in New York, especially Pierre Wertheimer.

After the liberation of France, she had been furious to learn that, for the entire length of the war, the Wertheimer brothers had been producing Chanel N°5 at their factory in Hoboken, New Jersey, having managed to get hold of the perfume's formula and find a stock of jasmine, which came via clandestine means from Grasse. She believed in her heart and soul that this version of N°5 was different, that it 'was not faithful', in her words. Her response was to have new perfumes made in Switzerland, which she did not market commercially but did distribute among her friends. Under the name 'Mademoiselle Chanel', she devised three of them: N°1, N°2 and N°31. She called these the *parfums rouges* ('red perfumes'), after the deep red label on the round bottle, against which the white lettering and numbers, designed by Tiny, stood out strikingly. These perfumes were more than a fleeting whim, for it was not in Coco's nature to get angry without letting it be known, especially with Pierre Wertheimer, whom she had always believed to be a friend.

In New York, Coco and Tiny were often invited to lunch with the Wertheimers. Tiny remembered the family atmosphere of these occasions, very much the opposite of the accounts circulated many years later, after Coco's death. Pierre had flowers sent to them at the Drake Hotel – white ones, of course – and Tiny was even sent bouquets of her own.

In 1947, an agreement was reached. Coco received damages for wartime sales of the American N°5; most importantly, she gave up her stake in the firm in return for comfortable royalties: 2 % on perfumes worldwide, or approximately one million US dollars per year. On top of this, her living costs would be paid, including the Ritz. 'From now on, I will no longer work,' she proclaimed in May 1947, little suspecting that she would one day reopen her couture house with the blessing and support of Pierre Wertheimer.

It was also in 1947, in Venice, that she met Louise de Vilmorin, 'one of the most prominent figures of post-war cultured society,'[172] and revived the idea of writing her memoirs. The two women arranged to work on this together at the rue Cambon, then various rewrites followed. Coco wanted to have the manuscript published in the USA so it could be adapted into a film. She went there in February 1948 to engage in negociations in person but returned without having made a deal. Soon afterwards, the writer Michel Déon made his own attempt at the delicate exercise of writing her memoirs. Unsurprisingly, given that the life she had dreamed up could not be faithfully transcribed, she was not satisfied with the results. The books by Louise de Vilmorin, Paul Morand and Michel Déon were not published until after her death.

It was during this era that she saw Paris revelling in the arrival of the New Look. It was now men – 'those gentle-men', as she called them – who called the shots in haute couture, with Christian Dior in the lead. Coco was sad to see the return of full skirts, wide-brimmed hats, tight waists, corsets and fitted bodices: all the hindrances she had battled against for a quarter of a century by embracing a minimalist kind of elegance and most of all by allowing greater freedom of movement.

She was there to see the triumphant success of Christian Dior, a near unknown of forty-two who had started out in fashion as a designer for Robert Piguet in 1938 and then began working with Lucien Lelong in 1941. In 1945, he had met Marcel Boussac, the 'Cotton King', and one of the richest men in France.

In 1946, financed by Boussac's millions and watched with curiosity by Paris society, Dior opened the couture house that bore his name and unveiled his first collection, 'Corolle', on 12 February 1947: a parade of flower-like women swathed in a profusion of fabrics, a clean break from the years of war and deprivation.

Dior lengthened skirts by 20 centimetres (8 inches). Seeing himself first and foremost as an architect, he resurrected the structural tricks of fashion: lined fabrics, petticoats to swell the skirts, boned bodices. He designed silhouettes with wasp waists and flaring hips; skirts were full, and bodices accentuated the décolletage.

It was a triumph. On 12 February 1947, the applause didn't stop at 20 avenue Montaigne. The 'Bar' suit was particularly admired, with its pleated black woollen skirt, using 12 metres (40 feet) of fabric and tulle underskirts to create a 'flower' effect, and with its peplum jacket in undyed silk shantung that cinched the waist. The influential Carmel Snow, editor-in-chief of *Harper's Bazaar*, exclaimed: 'Your dresses have such a new look!' The name stuck.

Christian Dior explained to a journalist: 'Fashion is like a flower, a beautiful blooming flower; that's what I thought about when making my next collection. The bust and, therefore, the face of women will be highlighted by a new cut that will give fullness to the body. I have always made it a rule to highlight, depending on the season, a particular attribute of the woman's body. Between us, isn't the bust the most seductive part? Of course, the waist remains slim, very slim. Isn't that every woman's dream?'[173]

Coco was poles apart from this discourse, this vision of decorative, fetishized, corseted femininity; Coco had worked with the sole aim of liberating women's bodies so they could take their place in society. An equal to men, the Chanel

Woman moves, breathes, creates, works, travels, plays sports and lives her life.

In public, however, Coco abstained from expressing an opinion, especially because of what she knew deep down in her surest soul: fashions pass, only style remains. She also knew that women would not give up the freedom they had fought so hard to attain. On the inside, however, she was indeed annoyed.

Her lack of employment was becoming burdensome, even though she absorbed herself in all sorts of pastimes every day: singing at the piano, playing the accordion, doing tarot readings – albeit in a way that allowed her to read only what she wanted to read – playing *belote*, and trying to contact the spirit world. But none of it was enough; her voracious soul demanded more. Of the five Chanel buildings on the rue Cambon, numbers 23, 25, 27 and 29 remained out of use; only number 31 was occupied. Tiny had set up a small workshop there, in one of the dusty rooms, to work on the scarf designs that Coco would ask her to produce: 'She told me to draw inspiration from the motifs on one of her lacquer screens – a bird, a flower, for example – or if not, to draw stars, suns, and interlocking double Cs.'[174]

Tiny had become Coco's confidant and had replaced her father, André, as Coco's object of obsession. For the first time, her nephew-son was rebelling, angry with the 'mother' he considered too possessive and intrusive. André was under no illusions: what he had to endure just to exist was considerable, and Coco's expectations were always too high. In 1949, he did not tell her about his remarriage – less than a year after his divorce – to Nina Kotzebue. Coco did not like this new wife and, as usual, made no secret of it.

Between Pierre Reverdy and Coco, things were much more calm. He continued writing to her and coming to see her. Their affection would last until they died. They often talked about prayer, God, nuns and monks, including Dom Aubourg, a monk they both knew.[175] In 1948, Reverdy came to bring her his last collection of poems, *Le Chant des morts*, illustrated with 125 lithographs by Picasso. It was a melancholy work, tackling the horror and darkness of war, as well as 'love, freedom in a too-empty sky'.

But poetry and prayers were no longer enough for Coco. Before the war, the all-consuming nature of her work had allowed her to keep the ghosts and hurt of the past at bay, to combine dreams and reality in visionary flights of fancy, to use her career as a kind of therapy. Now, however, in that period of retreat and anxious contemplation, everything came back to her: the scattered fragments of her life, her repressed pain. During those years of retirement, she listened to what her soul was telling her. Far from breaking her, the truth, which she faced head on, made her stronger. But the trials and tribulations still continued.

Since José María Sert's death in 1945, Coco had only seen Misia occasionally, although she still felt connected to her. Coco's aunt Adrienne and Misia remained Coco's closest friends, and while Coco would often visit the former, who led a quiet life on her property in Nexon, she was deeply saddened by the slow decline of the latter. Now partially blind – though able to see enough to shakily inject herself with regular doses of morphine – Misia was shrunken and sad. A sorrowful figure dressed in white, she floated through this world as though she already belonged to the next. The sight of her was sometimes unbearable for Coco, who considered it everyone's duty to retain their dignity and self-control. But it was mostly the presence of Boulos Ristelhueber, Misia's friend and secretary, that troubled her, as he had never been fond of Coco.

On 15 October 1950, as she was extending her summer stay in La Pausa, Coco was called to the bedside of the dying Misia. Other friends followed suit, including Cocteau. The day after Misia's death, Coco had her body laid on a four-poster bed and, for more than an hour, stayed with her behind closed doors, dressing her, combing her hair, doing her makeup, adorning her with jewels. When the doors opened, her friends could not help but let out a cry of admiration when they saw Misia lying radiant, as if her former beauty had been regained.

Coco told Tiny about these events but did not talk about her pain. 'She hated opening up, showing her feelings, and, even with me, if she ever let herself go for a moment, she would immediately pull herself back together by saying some-thing unpleasant, as if to wipe everything away.' However, when Adrienne died several years later, Coco did not try to hide her sadness: 'She was losing a friend and a sister, and I am one of the rare people to have witnessed the grief she felt that day.'[176]

In 1951, a figure suddenly returned from the ether: Walter Schellenberg. Released early from prison on the grounds of ill health, he was supported by Roger Masson, former chief of Swiss intelligence. Placed under the care of Dr Francis Lang in Billens, Switzerland, then transferred to a clinic in Pallanza on the shores of Lake Maggiore in Italy, where he was joined by his wife and children, the former head of German counterintelligence was attempting to write his memoirs, with help from the journalist Klaus Harpprecht. His aim was to emphasize his attempts at peacemaking, against Hitler's orders, and his efforts to save prisoners. He died not long afterwards, on 31 March 1952.

In his foreword to the German edition of Schellenberg's memoirs, Klaus Harpprecht mentioned some financial aid from 'a wealthy Frenchwoman in the cosmetics industry'.[177] He then said: 'This deliberately vague reference, born from a rumour propagated by Dr Francis Land, Schellenberg's physician, was not retained in later editions due to a lack of proof.'[178] This has been confirmed by Reinhard Doerries, Schellenberg's biographer.[179]

As for Dincklage, he returned to Germany in the early 1950s before moving to the Balearic Islands. Coco had long ago stopped seeing him. Although she no longer wanted any contact with him, he had played a part in helping some of her friends during the war (including Vera Lombardi), so true to her principles, she asked Tiny to send him some money.[180]

Two deaths cast a shadow over the year 1953. When Coco learned of the Duke of Westminster's passing, she decided to part with a reminder of that era of English elegance and splendour: La Pausa, her house in Roquebrune, which also held the unspeakably painful memories of Paul Iribe's tragic death on the tennis court. By a strange twist of fate, Winston Churchill continued to visit La Pausa, no longer to visit his friend the Duke of Westminster, but instead to see his literary agent, Emery Reves, who became the new owner.

In the same year, 1953, Coco lost Alphonse, the last of her five siblings. As the only surviving child of Albert Chanel and Jeanne Devolle, she chose to ignore the families of Alphonse and Lucien, to the point of never mentioning their existence in front of the only people she considered family: the Palasses. In 1954, she learned of the death of her beloved Étienne Balsan, with whom she had gradually lost touch after he went to live in Rio de Janeiro with his daughter Claude. He was hit by a car one day during Carnival. In mourning for her friend and his lifelong support, she could not help imagining the bloodstained road, the wounded body. Inevitably, she wept for Étienne and Boy as one.

As if unable to add those deaths to the others, as if compelled to push them away and try to wash away the pain by selling La Pausa and making another trip to America, Coco decided to regroup. Driven by a fierce desire to return to centre stage, to take on the new big names in fashion – Dior, Givenchy, Balenciaga and Fath, among others – she went to New York with an ulterior motive: to assess her chances of success. She saw Maggie van Zuylen at the Waldorf Astoria and also met with influential fashion journalists, including Carmel Snow from *Harper's Bazaar*, the same person who, several years earlier, had coined the name for Dior's New Look. In fact, at the sight of Maggie standing there in a green Dior dress that was beautiful but stifling, impeding her ability to breathe and move, Coco lost her temper. It was nothing but a step backwards, she thought.

French women had finally been granted the right to vote in 1944, but as soon as 1945 arrived, they were being taken back to the world of yesterday. In his speech on 2 March 1945, General de Gaulle spoke of the 'twelve million beautiful babies that France needs within ten years'. This obsession with giving birth pushed French women back into the home again, while a specific idea of feminine fashion designed by men – fitted waists and tight corsets – was becoming dominant. It was everything that Coco stood against.

The volcano awakened; the feminist within her roared, as did the class defector, who was not a prisoner of bourgeois ideas. Although it had been years since she had contemplated the idea, Coco decided to reopen her couture house. True to herself, she let her intuition be her guide. In 1953, at over seventy years old (although she said she was only sixty in order to avoid derogatory comments about her age), 'Mademoiselle' decided, with the ever-present support of Pierre Wertheimer, to reopen her couture house and her ateliers, to hire workers, and to design a new collection for release on a date that superstitiously included her lucky number – 5 February 1954.

11
THE EBONY PLAQUE

Dallas, Texas, USA, 1957. She listens to a barrage of compliments with a distracted ear. More than ever, in the salons of the Statler-Hilton Hotel, the memory of her father haunts her, her father who surely died here, in this land called America, the land he set off for on a winter's day in 1895 to try and make his fortune. This is merely her own version of the facts – that much is sure – but she has never had the heart to believe in another. Stanley Marcus, owner of Neiman Marcus stores, leans towards her to congratulate her and hands her an award, an ebony and silver plaque with an engraved inscription:

> 'To the great innovator who emancipated the feminine silhouette, who was the first to recognize that the casualness of the twentieth century must be reflected in the clothes that women wear, who elevated the status of costume jewelry to a position of fashionable respectability, who was the first to bring perfume from the chemist's shop to the couturier's boutique, who was never afraid of being copied, who as an ex-champion had the courage to stage a successful fashion comeback in 1954...'

Examining all those waiting faces, she thinks of all the hands she will have to shake next and tells herself they will never catch her there again.

> '...whose past accomplishments have had a tremendous influence on present fashions... To Chanel for her contributions past, present, and future,' Stanley Marcus concludes.

Applause ripples through the room. Coco forces a smile.

A day later, on 10 September 1957, Coco visited the ranch of Edward Marcus, Stanley's brother, in Lewisville. Unlike Elizabeth Arden, who sat next to her, Coco hated the barbecued meat and spicy beans she was served. But she was delighted by the 'fashion show' that closed the evening: a bull wearing a top hat and a cow with a feather boa around its neck and a veil on its head. 'These things', she said laughing, 'could only happen in America.' Stanley Marcus recalled: 'Mademoiselle Chanel seemed to be having a lot of fun, as did the many journalists who were following her.'[181] Although she was apprehensive about flying for the first time in her life, she had no regrets about making the trip. Stanley Marcus had been insistent; he wanted to give her the award in person.

When she reopened her fashion house after fourteen years of dormancy (1939–1953), the USA was the first to applaud her decision, while France grumbled that she was too old to go back into business. What's more, the couture designers who now occupied centre stage had no desire to share the spotlight.

'"There will never be a great woman designer," said Christian Dior. "We'll see about that!" replied Chanel', ran the headline in *Curieux*, a Neuchâtel newspaper, on 3 February 1954. The article went on to say: 'I don't know how Madeleine Vionnet or Jeanne Lanvin would have responded. But Chanel said, "We'll see about that." And she set her reopening for 5 February 1954.'

In reality, the welcome she received was far from warm. On 5 February, when she presented her collection, the Parisian press displayed 'atrocious contempt and malice', in the words of Michel Déon, who witnessed the debacle that day.[182] 'Hicksville chez Chanel', read the headline in *Combat*. 'It was sad; it was like it was 1925 again', commented *Le Figaro*. After the show, an awkward silence fell upon the rooms at the rue Cambon, while a misunderstood Mademoiselle hid herself away in her apartment. The collection, which opened with a suit in navy blue jersey, was deemed outdated and convinced no one. Despite being deeply hurt, Coco remained hopeful, believing that her creations would soon be embraced once again.

America, however, saw the Chanel look as timeless. The press praised her, the buyers rushed in; within a few months, her designs were being worn and copied. 'The Chanel look, as specific as H_2O, meant a combination of youth, comfort, jersey, pearls, of luxury hidden away in the perfection of detail,' enthused *Vogue* US on 15 February 1954. And on 1 March, *Life* exclaimed 'Chanel has lost none of her skill', before devoting several features to her.

With disarming spontaneity, Marilyn Monroe gave Chanel an unexpected advertising coup. 'What do you wear to bed?'

she was asked at a press conference. 'I only wear Chanel N°5,' she immediately replied. Her timeless response was published in the 7 April 1952 issue of *Life*, which featured Marilyn as its cover star for the first time. This burst of free publicity gave a huge boost to sales of N°5.

In the USA, Coco Chanel was already a living legend, but she was still waiting tirelessly for recognition from France, as she had done ever since her childhood and her father's abandonment. At over seventy years of age, she was still battling to promote her style, with its principles of comfort and freedom as well as those of sophistication and femininity, for which she had laid the foundations in the early 1910s. She loved to say: 'A woman can be over-dressed but never over-elegant.' Or: 'Elegance in clothing is the freedom to move.'

To achieve this remarkable harmony between the garment and the body – a harmony that made even her critical colleagues marvel – she would work directly on the model, cutting the fabric and inserting pins. Unlike most couturiers, she made no preliminary sketches. She gave instructions to the *première d'atelier*, and then the design was produced. Her style was established; she did not change silhouettes and skirt lengths every year, but instead chose to vary the colours and especially the fabrics, which were a great source of inspiration.

As soon as a pair of scissors on a white ribbon was hung around her neck, the ritual would begin. The model stepped out and slowly turned around, watched by her critical eye. From that moment on, she did not release her grip on the dress or the 'costume' (as she called a woman's suit). The long hours, and sometimes entire days, that followed were spent mumbling and commenting: 'I hate little nothings... Make me some pleats, but intelligent pleats... Cut it and let's stop talking about it...' The gazes that fell on her were respectful, often sideways rather than straight on, and sometimes fearful. Her monologues were punctuated by brief comments of 'Yes, Mademoiselle. Very good, Mademoiselle.'

She lightened and took away, cutting directly into even the most expensive fabrics, including fur. Fur, moreover, was only ever used inside garments, to add warmth, not to show off. 'Never a button without a buttonhole' was another of her sayings. She focused on details: a garment's interior had to be just as neat as its exterior. With the patience of an artisan, she could tirelessly take part and reassemble the same design fifteen or twenty times. As in the days of her Venetian adventures and her artistic education with José María Sert, she was in search of perfection at all costs.

And until she achieved it, she kept working 'Mademoiselle is sculpting a six-foot angel', Colette wrote. '...The unfinished angel sometimes trembles beneath those two creative, severe, kneading arms that press into her. Chanel works with her ten fingers, with her nails, with the edge of her hand, with her palm, with pins and with scissors, directly on the garment, which is a white mist with long pleats, scattered with cut crystals. Sometimes, she drops to her knees before her work and embraces it, not in reverence, but to punish it further, to fasten a cloud around the angel's long legs, to subdue some cloud of tulle.'[183]

Coco claimed that she 'could only work in anger', as if she were trying to 'punish' this image that would never be sufficiently perfect in her eyes. The harshness she sometimes displayed, by not accepting that others were tired or complaining that they wouldn't work on Sundays, was the same harshness that she inflicted on herself. Deep in pain, deep in sorrow, accustomed to death and misery, to the ungrateful ways of the earth and of men, she had been this way since 1895, when she was just twelve years old.

She worked even with a high fever and could not understand why others could not do the same. Even the pain in the joints of her right wrist did not slow her down; she simply bound it in a tight leather strap so she could continue wielding her scissors. She said: 'It was the artists who taught me rigour.' The results were as remarkable as her stubbornness. The clothes born from her hands became a second skin, seeming almost invisible, impalpable, intimate, so closely did they follow the movements of the body.

Coco rarely changed her suits; she only had three or four. She wore a boater (felt in winter, straw in summer), which she rarely took off, a silk chiffon scarf around her neck (to avoid catching a cold and end up coughing – or dying – like her mother) and a profusion of jewelry, most of which was costume. She kept her real jewels in simple white boxes that resembled shoeboxes, closed with a ribbon. Her makeup was outrageous, given that she had once preached the virtues of natural beauty; she accentuated her brows with a pencil, wore bold lipstick, and painted her nails.

In her bedroom and bathroom at the Ritz, her morning routine took some time. Tiny would often join her during these intimate moments, while Céline, the maid, would come and go. With her permission, Coco rechristened this woman 'Jeanne', like her mother.

Success finally arrived with her second comeback collection in 1954. Paris was at her feet. After the show, she went to see Pierre Wertheimer, put her arms around his neck and said simply: 'Thank you for everything, Pierre.' Pierre, who, 'through his associates, had pushed to amass the necessary capital',[184] was very touched.

The whole history of Coco's work was on dazzling display: the entire continuity of her style since the 1910s. And more so still in the famous Chanel suit, in which every detail was carefully thought out. The jacket moved with the body and then fell back into place naturally thanks to flexible fabrics, clever armholes, and a chain stitched into the lower hem of the lining, to add weight and balance. This comfortable base was adorned with patch pockets – for their look and practicality – plus braiding and jewel buttons, which provided a sense of femininity and sophistication. Two-tone pumps, beige with a black toe, and quilted shoulder bags added more touches of freedom. She named the collection '2.55' after the date of its creation. As for the dresses, they expressed the same sense of fluidity, movement and femininity. Coco favoured jersey, wild silk, tweed and chiffon, all lightweight fabrics; she also incorporated decorations into the fabric so as not to weigh down the garment. She loved floating panels and nude backs, which added sensuality. Everything was designed to create a natural allure.

She also expressed herself freely through accessories, which she had always deemed essential: a gold belt, a fabric camelia brooch, and a profusion of jewelry, both real and fake. Depending on the era, her jewelry was created in collaboration with Étienne de Beaumont, Fulco di Verdura, François Hugo, Suzanne Gripoix or Robert Goossens.

Goossens said that when he met Coco in 1957, she gave him books on antiquity, Byzantium, and the medieval era and they looked through them together in search of inspiration. She had always been drawn to classical or Byzantine jewelry. 'Why does everything I do become Byzantine?' she joked. She also asked him to draw inspiration from jewelry in museums, such as a Syrian bracelet from the Louvre, which she suggested he reinterpret. There were also the recurring motifs, 'her' motifs, the symbols of her childhood, especially the lion, the ear of wheat, the star and the cross. 'She was very religious and very mystic, we would talk about it together. Our conversations were easy; I would almost dare say we were on an equal footing since we knew that we both came from simple backgrounds. At the very beginning, however, I found myself disconcerted because she never gave direct compliments. When I asked her about it, she replied, "If it hadn't been good, I would have told you."'[185]

Coco daringly combined real gems and costume jewelry in a spirit of defiance and audacity, far removed from bourgeois posturing. She even combined them on the same pieces, including the brooch she often wore that incorporated diamonds alongside imitation rubies and emeralds.

This did not prevent the Chanel style from being embraced by the bourgeoisie, nor by the people in the street. *Elle* magazine, edited by Hélène Lazareff, a client and fervent admirer of Coco, regularly featured Chanel on its covers, and Chanel suits were worn by many prominent women. 'It reassures me when my wife is dressed by you,' President Pompidou confided to Coco during a dinner at the Élysée Palace. The remark amused her, but she did not make a big deal of it. On 22 November 1963, the whole world saw the blood of the assassinated US president on Jackie Kennedy's pink tweed Chanel suit, a scene that would take on a mythical dimension.

Dressing the great and the good was flattering to Coco, but it was not her primary goal. What she had her sights set on was more democratic: it was about freedom and the bodies of women, all women, starting with herself. Historian Michelle Perrot stresses: 'Coco Chanel turned everything into freedom. She was a pioneer, a rebel who definitely played a part in the emancipation of women. Even those – the majority – who could not afford Chanel clothes felt freed from more elaborate and restrictive fashions. But because she was a rebel, Coco Chanel made people uncomfortable, and paid a price for her attitude, her freedom at a time when these things were frowned upon in women. Like all exceptional women, she cannot escape from myth-making, which obscures her most unusual traits and reduces them to stereotypes. We care little about her real story.'[186]

Coco was delighted to see that her style had been embraced by the streets, that it had been copied, that was inspiring: 'That's what I tried to do. It was my goal to create a style.' At the time of her big comeback, she told the American press: 'I am no longer interested in dressing a few hundred women, private clients; I shall dress thousands of women.'[187] The little black dress, the jersey ensemble, or the tweed suit: these were items that simplified the lives of women, all women. First and foremost, they were ideas and concepts: timeless femininity and modernity.

She was once again asked to design costumes for films, and dressed Jeanne Moreau in *Les Amants* by Louis Malle, followed by Delphine Seyrig in *Last Year in Marienbad* by Alain Resnais. Luchino Visconti commissioned her to design costumes for *Boccaccio '70* and asked her, among other things, to mentor the young Romy Schneider and teach her elegance.

On the French TV show *Cinq Columns à la Une*, which aired on 6 February 1959, she projected a curious combination of self-assurance and vulnerability. She explained to Pierre Dumayet: 'The human body moves all the time, so you need clothes that follow the movement. Take me, for instance, right now I'd like to stop moving and speak calmly. It's very difficult for me.'

Indeed, her body can be seen twisting left and right, shifting her weight from one foot to the other, her head jerking, her gaze falling and rising. Then her whole body tips forwards, her right arm coming up to rub the nape of her neck. This extreme nervousness, the body that ached and moved, even when she didn't want it to, the fire that consumed her: this was the secret to her unrelenting ability to work. It was not in her nature to live on the road like her father but she was nonetheless in perpetual motion. Looking at her, you might think that if she ever stopped moving, she would die.

Pierre Reverdy died in Solesmes in June 1960. Afterwards, Coco declared: 'Poets, you know, are not like us; they do not die.' This loss drove her to become more absorbed than ever in her work at the rue Cambon. She liked to make herself part of everyone's life – models, colleagues – and give advice, not only on being elegant but also on how to behave.

Jean Mermod, who, at the time, represented Chanel perfumes and beauty products in Switzerland, remembered seeing her jump up, scissors in hand, and leap towards a friend, the wife of her Swiss dentist, in order to cut open the sleeve of her suit and take out the unnecessary padding.[188] She regularly acted in this way. On one occasion, she took apart the back and shoulder of a model's own suit, thinking it was poorly cut, while ignoring its owner's squeals; on another, she unpicked the sleeve of a Chanel suit worn by an American guest at the Ritz. She did not bother to ask the opinion of the ladies concerned, believing that any fault should be fixed on the spot.

In her later years, Coco no longer understood the times she was living in. She loathed short dresses and miniskirts: 'Knees are rarely beautiful on a woman, so why show them? It's like showing off your elbows.' She loathed the little tops that left very little concealed: 'When everything is revealed, there is nothing left to desire.' She even criticized trousers, a fashion she herself had kickstarted in the 1920s: 'I invented them out of modesty. After a dip in the sea, you might as well put on trousers. A skirt isn't pretty, a bathrobe is awful. But to go from that to making a fashion out of it and having seventy percent of ladies at a dinner party in trousers, that's quite sad.'

But mostly, it was the times that Coco detested – the 'yeah-yeah era' as she called it – as well as her own loneliness and regrets. 'In the end, Tiny, you're the one who's right. You have a husband, children, and I am alone,' she confided on one occasion.[189] Publicly she said, in a cracked voice: 'A woman who is not loved is a useless woman.'

In the 1960s, she led a monastic life. But Coco had been going to bed early and going out very rarely for quite some time. 'If I told people how you live, people wouldn't believe me,' Cocteau had once joked, back in the Faubourg-Saint-Honoré days.

Every day, she arrived at the rue Cambon at around half-past twelve. She had the luxury of having a permanent cook and being able to invite anyone she pleased to her apartments. One day in the boutique, Coco noticed a young woman she did not recognize, choosing a scarf and holding a book under her arm. 'You're lucky you have the time to read,' she said to the woman, whose name was Claude Delay-Tubiana, before inviting her to lunch the following day.

She delighted in this chance encounter – having always loved the workings of fate – because apart from her family and business associates, she had very few close friends left in this world, especially since the few survivors 'never seemed to be free', she often said with a sigh.

But the Palasses were still around. Coco often went to the Île Saint-Louis, where Tiny lived with her husband Jacques and their two sons, Guillaume and Pierre-Hugues. She would announce that she was coming 'for tea', although this was just an excuse, since she despised tea. She liked to invite Guillaume and Pierre-Hugues for meals at the rue Cambon, either together or separately. 'She is very present and loving with them,' Tiny said, pleased. Conversely, she less frequently visited Goupillières in Normandy, to see André and his wife Nina, since she did not like the latter.

She began to sort out, throw away and burn things more than usual. She had Boy's furniture – the Chinese cabinet and throne base – sent to Tiny. Shortly afterwards, she solemnly gave Boy's notebook to Tiny too, as well as a folder which she asked her to keep, containing documents letters, and photographs.

Coco wrote her will in 1965. It can be summed up in a few words: 'I leave all that I own to my Coga Foundation. Lausanne, 11 October 1965. Gabrielle Chanel.' She explained to Tiny: 'This way, you won't have any problems when I die. Everything will be settled, and you won't run the risk of being hounded by parasites.' The Coga foundation (for Coco-Gabrielle), with its headquarters in Liechtenstein, was instructed to pay out regular allowances. These would go to Coco's family, of course, and to friends and artists, but also to people who had faithfully worked with her over the years, either in the ateliers or as servants. This new will came as a surprise to André, since, until then, he had been Coco's sole heir, but he came to see the sense in Coga. Serge Lifar, on the other hand, only became aware of these provisions after Coco's death. Having expected to receive something, he flew into an angry rage and started spreading nasty rumours about the late Coco's activities during the Occupation.[190]

In 1966, Coco bought what she called her 'little Swiss house' and told Tiny that she wanted to be buried in Lausanne. Switzerland remained her refuge; she went there often. It was via the concierge at the Lausanne Palace that she found her new residence, on high ground, surrounded by trees. When Jean Mermod pointed out that the house was nothing special, she retorted: 'But it has good bones, that's what counts,' and added, 'Anyway, I'm going to cover it in wood and turn it into a chalet.'[191] She never did this, for the good reason that she only stayed there occasionally (although she did install a wrought iron gate decorated with wheat-ear motifs). The house at 22 route du Signal, perched above Lausanne's chateau, cathedral and old town, sat at the end of a narrow road that ran between two neat hedges and two rows of trees. These aspects appealed to Coco, as did the promixity to woodland. Like a bridge between two worlds, connecting her present with her childhood, this place became her final home and would be listed as such on her death certificate.

She often called Switzerland a 'clean country', saying 'it feels safe there', that 'everything works, and the people there are serious'. On one occasion, she gave some thought to presenting a collection in Lausanne, in order to 'teach Paris a lesson' and demonstrate that Paris was not the centre of the world, but she soon forgot the idea. After all, the rue Cambon was her lifetime achievement.

When evening fell, Coco's loneliness was becoming increasingly hard to bear. She worked long hours and, when preparing a collection, would keep her models around until nine or nine-thirty at night, along with her friends, collaborators and employees. Lilou Marquand, her faithful assistant, and François Mironnet, her *maître d'hôtel*, often found themselves playing cards behind closed doors to keep Mademoiselle happy.

As for Claude Delay-Tubiana, she sometimes came to the rooms at the Ritz for dinner, where Coco would greet her in white silk pyjamas. 'I always felt guilty leaving, abandoning her, gripped by that awful dread of loneliness,' she recounts. 'When François Mironnet left for four days without explanation, not daring to say he was going on his honeymoon, Coco felt terribly abandoned, just as she had in her orphanage days, and then, just once, I saw her give herself several injections of Sedol.'[192]

François, of course, was more than a *maître d'hôtel*. In the evening, she often asked him to take off his white gloves, dine with her, listen to her. She suggested that he work for her in jewelry, as she had detected a certain artistic skill in him, and also offered him weight-loss cures, since he disliked being overweight. He always carried neatly folded notes to pay bills and give tips.

When her longtime lawyer, René de Chambrun, flew off for a long vacation with his wife, Coco once again felt abandoned. 'I'm going to get a younger one,' she announced; this would be Robert Badinter. René de Chambrun had been introduced to Coco in 1934 through Baron van Zuylen, and she became the young lawyer's first business client. He was, of course, the son-in-law of former French prime minister Pierre Laval, having married his only daughter in 1935, but he was also a direct descendant of the Marquis de Lafayette and had dual French-American nationality. Once Coco loved or trusted someone, she was steadfast. She had been loyal to

René de Chambrun, who had protected her interests since 1934, and would be loyal to Robert Badinter for the last seven years of her life.[193] She showed this same loyalty to her Swiss banker, whom she nicknamed Mathusalem.

She would only open up to her few close friends, preferring to deluge others with invented stories about her life and tales of the flamboyant days when the Duke of Westminster had been courting her. Coco could speak non-stop about the Swinging Sixties, an era that she could not understand, and although she talked mostly about herself, this did not mean she was letting people in. 'I prefer to pay not to be alone', she admitted. 'You might as well surround yourself with scoundrels you can have fun with rather than people who are good but boring.'[194] Towards the end of her life, she certainly feared boredom, but what she feared even more was being too clear-minded. Never fooled by anything, always on her guard, guessing the truth of people before they revealed themselves: it was all exhausting. She dreamed, in sad comparison, of the years between the wars, when she had rubbed shoulders with great artists.

This may well have been what led her to grant permission in 1969 for a musical entitled *Coco*, especially since the proposal came from America; it came from the team behind *My Fair Lady*, with a libretto by Alan Jay Lerner, costumes by Cecil Beaton, and Katharine Hepburn in the lead role. Coco invited Lerner and Frederick Brisson, the producer, to the rue Cambon to talk about the project, but claimed to trust them enough not to read the script. Sitting in her usual surroundings – upright, never languid, and always on the alert – habitually smoothing her skirt over her knees with the flat of her hand, her hat perched over her thick fringe of hair, she listened to what they had to say. The musical promised to be one of the most expensive in Broadway history. Coco was already thinking of the gown that Katharine Hepburn might wear for the premiere, one of those gowns she was so skilled at creating, of silk chiffon or lamé in the most delicate of shades.

Her left hand came to rest, in another customary gesture, on a meteorite mounted on a pedestal, one of her favourite objects, unearthed in London in the shop of an antique dealer who specialized in Chinese art: 'I cannot sell it to you', the man had explained to her, 'I'm going to give it to you because one does not sell an object fallen from the sky.'

A few days before the premiere, in December 1969, while her suite at the Waldorf Astoria was awaiting her, her gowns at the ready, she woke up at the rue Cambon with her right hand paralysed. She had already spent several weeks wondering if this trip to America was worthwhile: it would be one of her last, she thought, given her eighty-seven years. The doctor's diagnosis was a compression of the radial nerve, also known as 'Saturday night palsy'. Despite herself, the term made her smile. Her trip was cancelled, with no regrets. Certainly, America had given her a lot, but hadn't it also 'stolen away' her father? For nearly two months, her hand remained unresponsive, supported by a black elasticated wrist strap with gold decoration, and for the first time she realized how much her staff loved her, because they all pretended not to notice.

A short time later, in 1970, she launched a new perfume that became her favourite: Chanel N°19. The 19 represented her birthday and her father's birthday. With its green, floral notes, it evoked youth and nature. A way to reconnect with childhood and bring the Absent One to life.

In those last months, whenever she read Reverdy to those close to her, as she had always loved to do, her voice no longer trembled.

Erase smother the image the memory
the noise
Hear nothing more
nor see

12
THE FIVE
STONE LIONS

Hotel Ritz, Paris, France, Sunday, 10 January 1971. Coco, modest as ever, is standing in front of her dressing table in her petticoat, her arms bare, when Claude Delay-Tubiana comes into the room. 'I had always seen her in a suit and, for the first time, because of her wrinkled arms, I realized that she was an old lady. Yet at the same time, she had so much ardour, so much intensity!'[195]

In her room beneath the roof of the Ritz, Coco stands motionless, her gaze fixed for a brief moment, and murmurs, without turning to Claude: 'Tomorrow, I won't be able to resist the urge the make that dress with a bustle that my mother wore.' Then the flood of words resumes and she moves once again, making hundreds of suggestions for the afternoon.

Soon she is dressed in a tweed suit with pink silk braid, a hat and makeup – even on her hands, since she applies foundation and powder to them – and glitters with jewels laid out by Jeanne the maid: the metamorphosis is complete.

Her favourite spot is waiting for her at the edge of the dining room, away from the cooking smells and the pathways followed by the waiters, and closer to the hallway, so she can watch people coming in and see what they are wearing, which she likes to do. 'Mr Ritz' comes over to greet them.

Coco orders her usual well-chilled Riesling. Lunch will never last as long as it does on that day.

After giving instructions to her driver – her 'mechanic', as she insists on calling him – she leans back and makes herself comfortable. She used to own a Rolls-Royce, but one day, she was startled by a reflection of herself in the window, a frail silhouette in the back seat – she thought she was seeing a vision of her own funeral. And so she sold the Rolls in favour of a black Cadillac.

Arriving at the racecourse with Claude, her favourite place, she asks her driver to pause only for a moment. Without stepping out of the car, she tells them about the smell of horses, and the haunting sense of times gone by. When her long monologue ends, a shiver runs up her spine. She tucks her little cashmere blanket around herself.

Passing the Museum of Modern Art on the way back, she talks about her friend Dalí and the painting he once gave her, showing an ear of wheat on a black background. This is one of the few pictures she owns. In the end, she never really developed a love of paintings, except for Picasso.

She has the Cadillac stop just outside the doors of the Ritz. Turning, she says to Claude: 'Don't come to lunch tomorrow, I'm working.' From behind, she looks even more frail in her little tweed coat with its fur lining.

In her room, she takes off her suit jacket with help from Jeanne the maid. She sits on the edge of the bed in a simple skirt and blouse, automatically checking the objects on her bedside table: the icon painting, the bouquet of white flowers, next to Paul Morand's *Milady* and Johann Peter

Eckermann's book of his conversations with Goethe. As she rings downstairs to order her dinner, she suddenly lets out a cry, holding her stomach in pain. Frightened, Jeanne calls Lilou straight away. Jeanne, who is now Céline once more, hears Coco's last words: 'This is how you die.'

Tiny and her sister Hélène soon arrive. They watch over the body and block the door. Coco had asked for nobody to see her on her deathbed, but they nonetheless allow two of her most loyal employees to help watch over her.

She had wanted to die in Switzerland, and to be buried there, as quietly as possibly. She was indeed buried in the cemetery in Lausanne, but the funeral took place at the Church of La Madeleine in Paris, in the presence of the seamstresses, models and other employees of the House of Chanel, as well as friends and other important people. Only afterwards would she be taken to her Swiss cemetery, as peaceful as those of her childhood, planted with bushes and trees.

Coco, who had planned everything in advance, had asked Jacques, Tiny's husband, to design her tomb, with its five sculpted lions' heads, those beloved symbols that had stayed with her throughout her life and now accompanied her in death. In addition, she had a small stone bench installed nearby so that people could come and talk to her, or listen to her.

She hadn't wanted a slab, just a headstone above a bed of white flowers. 'That way,' she used to say, 'I can come back out if I feel like it.'

She truly believed that she could.

Notes

1   Conversations with Gabrielle Palasse-Labrunie, 1996–2014.

2   Adrien Alphonse Chanel was born on 11 September 1881, and died 11 November 1881 in Saintes; municipal archives of Saintes.

3   Conversations with Gabrielle Palasse-Labrunie, 1996–2014.

4   'Rumours in Courpière kept this memory alive for a century. Let us admire the memory of villages', wrote Colette Valaude ('Gabrielle Coco Chanel. Courpière ou l'enfance reniée', in *Courpière, porte du Livradois-Forez*, published by the City of Courpière, 1998, p. 265). I would also like to thank Colette and Paul Valaude for the valuable help they gave to me in 1996–1997 during my early research in Courpière and Issoire.

5   Marriage certificate dated 17 November 1884, municipal archives of Courpière.

6   Marriage certificate dated 17 November 1884, municipal archives of Courpière.

7   Municipal archives of Courpière.

8   Conversations with Gabrielle Palasse-Labrunie, 1996–2014.

9   Sentenced on 23 June 1883, by the magistrates' court of Tours. Departmental archives of Indre-et-Loire.

10   Municipal archives of Saumur, departmental archives of Maine-et-Loire. Only one first name is listed on her birth certificate: 'Gabrielle'. On her baptism certificate, the first names 'Jeanne Gabrielle' appear. There is no record of the

name 'Gabrielle Bonheur', which, although mentioned by some biographers, is pure invention. Her close friends called her Coco; everyone else called her Gabrielle.

11   The archives are now mostly digitized and available online, but this was not the case in around 1996, when I first began my research. At the time, I had to locate all the documents via letters and in-person trips. I gave a copy of this file to Gabrielle Palasse-Labrunie because Coco Chanel deliberately retained very few documents.

12   Conversations with Gabrielle Palasse-Labrunie, 1996–2014.

13   The incorrect name of Charnet was replaced by Chanel, the true surname, by judgment of the Court of First Instance of Nîmes on 21 January 1878; municipal archives of Nîmes, departmental archives of Gard.

14   Land registry and notarial deeds, municipal archives of Courpière, departmental archives of Puy-de-Dôme, for the Devolle and Chardon houses. For the Devolle house, the deed of ownership was provided by the current owner to Mrs Colette Valaude, private archives.

15   Conversations with Gabrielle Palasse-Labrunie, 1996–2014.

16   Death certificate of Jeanne Devolle, municipal archives of Brive-la-Gaillarde.

17   Conversations with Gabrielle Palasse-Labrunie, 1996–2014.

18   Interview with Laurent Puech, who also collected the correspondence of the Chanel children. Musée Cévenol, Le Vigan.

19   Interview with Adrienne Valet, daughter of Marie-Louise Voisse and Hippolyte Chanel, in Pierre Galante, *Les Années Chanel*, p. 135.

20   As noted in 1972 by Edmonde Charles-Roux, Gaston Defferre, mayor of Marseille, and Marie-Rose Guillot, curator of the Brive-la-Gaillarde Museum. Their letters were entrusted to me in 1999.

21 1896 census, Thiers, rue Durolle, departmental archives
    of Puy-de-Dôme. See also: Henri Ponchon, *L'Enfance
    de Chanel*, Saint-Pourçain-sur-Sioule: Bleu Autour,
    2016, p. 103.

22 Conversations with Gabrielle Palasse-Labrunie, 1996–2014.

23 Conversations with Gabrielle Palasse-Labrunie. See also:
    '*Mon père m'amait* (My father loved me)' in Louise de
    Vilmorin, *Mémoires de Coco*, p. 48, and '*Moi, il m'aimait
    bien* (He loved me a lot)', in Marcel Haedrich, *Coco Chanel
    secrète*, p. 38.

24 Louise de Vilmorin, *Memoirs de Coco*, p. 45.

25 Paul Morand, *The Allure of Chanel* (1976), illustrated by
    Karl Lagerfeld, London: Pushkin Press, 2013, p. 24.

26 Marcel Haedrich, *Coco Chanel secrète*, p. 53.

27 *Le Moniteur d'Issoire*, 6 April and 17 August 1898.
    Municipal archives of Issoire.

28 1911 census, Quimper, departmental archives of Finistère.

29 Wedding of Antoinette Chanel and Oscar Édouard Fleming,
    11 November 1919, in the 8th arrondissement of Paris,
    Paris archives.

30 Conversations with Gabrielle Palasse-Labrunie,
    1996–2014.

31 1997 interview with Dominique Legrand, bursar of the
    establishment for twenty-five years, during which she
    had the opportunity to talk about Coco Chanel with the
    oldest of the nuns. Registers and other archives have not
    been preserved.

32 Conversations with Gabrielle Palasse-Labrunie, 1996–2014.

33 Conversations with Gabrielle Palasse-Labrunie, 1996–2014.

34 'It happened that a large number of people who were close to
    Mademoiselle wondered whether André Palasse could be her
    son.' Letter from Georges Madoux to René de Chambrun,
    12 April 1972, private archives.

35 On Albert Chanel's birth certificate, there is no marginal
    note to indicate death. 'The civil records officer of the place
    of death did not notify his counterpart in Nîmes,' a clerk at
    the Gard departmental archives confirmed to me.

36 The Bhagavad Gita, Chapter VII ('On Divine Knowledge'),
    verse 27.

37 Interviews with Quitterie Tempé, granddaughter of Étienne
    Balsan, in April 2006, then April–May 2010.

38 Paul Morand, *Lewis and Irene*, New York: Boni & Liveright,
    1925, pp. 12, 47, and 82.

39 Conversations with Gabrielle Palasse-Labrunie, 1996–2014.

40 The Bhagavad Gita, Chapter III ('On Action'), verse 19.

41 Paul Morand, *The Allure of Chanel*, edited and illustrated
    by Karl Lagerfeld, London: Pushkin Press, 2013, p. 48.

42 Conversations with Gabrielle Palasse-Labrunie, 1996–2014
    and interviews with Claude Delay-Tubiana, 1997–1998.

43 Death certificate of Arthur Edward Capel. Municipal archives
    of Fréjus.

44 Conversations with Gabrielle Palasse-Labrunie, 1996–2014.

45 Guillaume Labrunie was born in 1957 and died on 9 April 2023.
    Pierre-Hugues was born in 1959 and died in 1988. Guillaume
    had one daughter, Marine.

46 Arthur Gold and Robert Fizdale, *Misia: The Life of Misia Sert*,
    New York: Morrow Quill, 1981, p. 198.

47 Arthur Gold and Robert Fizdale, *Misia: The Life of Misia Sert*,
    p. 197.

48 Lisa Chaney, *Chanel: An Intimate Life* [2011], London:
    Penguin, 2012, p. 169.

49 Interview with Jacques Polge, 25 March 2015; Polge was the
    'nose' of the House of Chanel from 1978 to 2014. He was the
    house's third perfumer after Ernest Beaux and Henri Robert.

50 Named after the two artistic centres of Paris, Montmartre and
    Montparnasse, the magazine published work by new artistic

movements, including talents such as Max Jacob, Aragon, Breton, Tristan Tzara, Apollinaire, and, in graphic art, Léger, Derain, Braque, and Juan Gris.

51 Personal archives.
52 Michel Leiris, in *Pierre Reverdy, 1889–1960,* ed. Maurice Saillet, Paris: Mercure de France, 1962, p. 130.
53 *Les Lettres françaises*, Paris, 23 June 1960, no. 830.
54 Maurice Sachs, *Au temps du bœuf sur le toit* [1939], Paris: Grasset, 'Les Cahiers rouges', 1989, p. 103.
55 Personal archives.
56 Personal archives.
57 Conversations with Gabrielle Palasse-Labrunie, 1996–2014.
58 Personal archives.
59 Maurice Sachs, *Au temps du bœuf sur le toit*, p. 224.
60 *Ibid.*, pp. 223–224.
61 *Ibid.*, p. 234.
62 *The New York Times*, 5 March 1931.
63 Personal archives.
64 Personal archives.
65 Pierre Reverdy, 'Toi ou moi', in *Sources du vent* [1929], Paris, Gallimard, 1998, p. 113
66 Conversations with Gabrielle Palasse-Labrunie, 1996–2014.
67 Personal archives.
68 Conversations with Gabrielle Palasse-Labrunie, 1996–2014.
69 Conversations with Gabrielle Palasse-Labrunie, 1996–2014.
70 Interview with Sophie Kurkdjian, fashion and media historian, and researcher at the IHTP (Institut d'Histoire du Temps Présent), 12 April 2022.
71 *Vogue* Paris, September 1938.
72 Personal archives.
73 Personal archives.
74 Conversations with Gabrielle Palasse-Labrunie, 1996–2014.
75 Personal archives.

76   Personal archives.

77   Personal archives.

78   Personal archives.

79   Dominique Veillon, *Fashion Under the Occupation*, trans. Miriam Kochan, Oxford and New York: Berg Publishers, 2002, pp. 132–134.

80   Elsa Schiaparelli, *Shocking Life*, New York: Dutton, 1954, p. 150

81   Dominique Veillon, *Fashion Under the Occupation*, 2002, p. VIII.

82   Dominique Veillon, *Fashion Under the Occupation*, 2002, p. 106.

83   French National Archives, F/7/15299.

84   Dominique Veillon, *Fashion Under the Occupation*, 2002, p. VIII.

85   Personal archives.

86   Service Historique de la Défense (French Ministry of Defence archives), territorial network department, Cherbourg division, Fonds Amiot, 5N4.

87   Letters stored at the Musée du Vigan and collected by Laurent Puech.

88   Receipt found in the Madoux papers. See Jean Lebrun (who met Mrs Madoux in 1989) in *Notre Chanel*, Saint-Pourçain-sur-Sioule: Bleu Autour, 2014, p. 225. As usual, Coco did not keep the receipt herself.

89   Interviews with Quitterie Tempé, granddaughter of Étienne Balsan, in April 2006, then April–May 2010.

90   Statement by André Cousso, former mayor of Auga, municipal bulletin.

91   Conversations with Gabrielle Palasse-Labrunie, 1996–2014.

92   Jean Marais, *Histoires de ma vie* [1975], Paris: Albin Michel, 1998, p. 118.

93   Conversations with Gabrielle Palasse-Labrunie, 1996–2014.

94   Arthur Gold and Robert Fizdale, *Misia: The Life of Misia Sert*, New York: Morrow Quill, 1981, p. 290.

95   Conversations with Gabrielle Palasse-Labrunie, 1996–2014.
96   Service Historique de la Défense (French Ministry of
     Defence archives), 7NN 2973.
97   Service Historique de la Défense, GR 28 P9 and 7NN 2973.
98   Service Historique de la Défense, GR 28 P9 and 7NN 2973.
99   Service Historique de la Défense, GR 28 P9 and 7NN 2973.
100 Service Historique de la Défense, GR 28 P9 and 7NN 2973.
101 Service Historique de la Défense, GR 28 P9 and 7NN 2973.
102 Service Historique de la Défense, GR 28 P9.
103 Service Historique de la Défense, GR 28 P9 and 7NN 2973.
104 Archives of the Paris Police Prefecture, 77 W 2027 / No. 393.856
105 Service Historique de la Défense, GR 28 P9 and 7NN 2973.
106 British Intelligence Report on the Case of Walter Schellenberg,
     File XE001752, Investigative Records Repository, Records of the
     Army Staff, Record Group 319, US National Archives at College
     Park, Maryland. These archives were declassified in 1987.
107 French National Archives, F/7/15327, General Intelligence
     Directorate files, 'Feihl, press attaché at the German Embassy',
     p. 122.
108 Maurice Garçon, *Journal, 1939–1945*, Paris: Les Belles Lettres/
     Fayard, 2015, p. 177; reprinted in paperback in the 'Tempus'
     series, Perrin, 2017.
109 Conversations with Gabrielle Palasse-Labrunie, 1996–2014.
110 French National Archives, AJ/40/871.
111 Conversations with Gabrielle Palasse-Labrunie, 1996–2014.
112 Service Historique de la Défense, GR 28 P9.
113 French National Archives, Z/6762 Registry 5559.
114 French National Archives, Z/6762 Registry 5559.
115 Service Historique de la Défense, 7NN 2717.
116 Service Historique de la Défense, 7NN 2717.
117 French National Archives, Z/6762 Registry 5559.
118 Service Historique de la Défense, 7NN 2717.
119 Service Historique de la Défense, 7NN 2717.

120 Service Historique de la Défense, 7NN 2717.

121 Service Historique de la Défense, GR 28 P9.

122 French National Archives, Z/6762 Registry 5559.

123 French National Archives, Z/6762 Registry 5559.

124 French National Archives, Z/6762 Registry 5559.

125 Archives of the Police Prefecture, BA 1990.

126 Service Historique de la Défense, GR 28 P9.

127 Service Historique de la Défense, GR 28 P9

128 British National Archives, 1139.

129 Conversations with Gabrielle Palasse-Labrunie, 1999–2014.

130 Introduction to the *Inventaire des archives du Commissariat général aux questions juives* (*Inventory of the Archives of the General-Commissariat for Jewish Affairs*), French National Archives.

131 *Ibid.*

132 Service Historique de la Défense, territorial network department, Cherbourg division, Fonds Amiot 5N4.

133 27 April 2022 interview with Lucile Chartain, head of the AJ/38 collection at the French National Archives, Executive and Legislative Department, World Wars division.

134 'Les parfums Chanel, Neuilly-sur-Seine', French National Archives, Collection of the General-Commissariat for Jewish Affairs (CGQJ) and the Service for the Restitution of Looted Property, AJ38/2 725, file 945. This source can be consulted on microfilm: MIC/AJ/38/2 725.

135 *Ibid.*

136 Introduction to the Inventory of the Archives of the General Commission for Jewish Affairs (CGQJ), National Archives.

137 'Les parfums Chanel, Neuilly-sur-Seine', French National Archives, Collection of the General-Commissariat for Jewish Affairs (CGQJ) and the Service for the Restitution of Looted Property, AJ38/2 725, file 945. This source can be consulted on microfilm: MIC/AJ/38/2 725.

138 *Ibid.*
139 Service Historique de la Défense, territorial network
     department, Cherbourg division, Fonds Amiot 5N4.
140 'Les parfums Chanel, Neuilly-sur-Seine', French National
     Archives, General Commission for Jewish Affairs (CGQJ)
     and Service for the Restitution of Looted Property, AJ38/2 725.
     File 945. This source can be consulted on microfilm:
     MIC/AJ/38/2 725.
141 Service Historique de la Défense, territorial network
     department, Cherbourg division, Fonds Amiot 5N4.
142 'Les parfums Chanel, Neuilly-sur-Seine', French National
     Archives, General Commission for Jewish Affairs (CGQJ)
     and Service for the Restitution of Looted Property, AJ38/2 725.
     File 945. This source can be consulted on microfilm:
     MIC/AJ/38/2 725.
143 2015 interview with Monique Leblois-Péchon, head of the
     AJ/38 collection at the French National Archives until 2016.
144 'Les parfums Chanel, Neuilly-sur-Seine', French National
     Archives, General Commission for Jewish Affairs (CGQJ)
     and Service for the Restitution of Looted Property,
     AJ38/2 725. File 945. This source can be consulted
     on microfilm: MIC/AJ/38/2 725.
145 *Ibid.*
146 Service Historique de la Défense, territorial network
     department, Cherbourg division, Fonds Amiot 5N4.
147 *Ibid.*
148 *Ibid.*
149 Conversations with Gabrielle Palasse-Labrunie, 1996–2014.
150 Personal archives.
151 Author's correspondence from 1998, with Reinhard R.
     Doerries, German intelligence specialist and biographer
     of Walter Schellenberg.
152 Dominique Veillon, *Fashion Under the Occupation*, p. 72.

153   Lilou Marquand, *Chanel m'a dit...*, Paris: JC Lattès, 1990, p. 114.
154   British Intelligence Report on the Case of Walter Schellenberg.
       File XE0011752. Investigative Records Repository, Records of
       the Army Staff, Record Group 319, US National Archives at
       College Park, Maryland. These archives, declassified in 1987,
       were published in *Hitler's Last Chief of Foreign Intelligence:
       Allied Interrogations of Walter Schellenberg*, London &
       Portland, OR: F. Cass, 2003. This original report contains
       the only mention (on page 65) of Coco's visit to Berlin. Other
       sources (French National Archives and British National
       Archives) mention only a trip to Madrid. This may be a
       mistake on the part of Schellenberg: the fact that his story
       contained inconsistencies was discussed by his interrogators.
       In addition, the date he gives is not correct: 'April 1944'
       instead of 'late 1943'.
155   The Sir Winston Churchill Archive Trust & Content.
       CHAR 20/198A. (Gabrielle Palasse-Labrunie had a copy of
       this letter.) The letter is dated 10 January 1944, according to
       embassy records.
156   Interview with Sir Stuart Hampshire, at his home in Oxford,
       20 October 1998.
157   Service Historique de la Défense, GR 28 P9.
158   French National Archives, Z/6762 Registry 5559.
159   French National Archives, F/7/14939.
160   Malcolm Muggeridge, *Chronicles of Wasted Time:
       An Autobiography*, vol. 2, London: Collins, 1973, p. 242.
161   May 2015 correspondence with Sally Muggeridge and
       David Malone.
162   Service Historique de la Défense, territorial network
       department, Cherbourg division, Fonds Amiot 5N4.
163   French National Archives, Z/6762 Registry 5559.
164   Interviews with Pascal Raimbault, head of document review,
       French Department of Justice and the Interior, French

National Archives, May 2016.

165 French Ministry of the Interior.

166 French Ministry of the Interior.

167 With special permission, I previously published excerpts from these interrogations in *Chanel. L'énigme*, Paris: Flammarion, 2016.

168 Henri Michaux, *Lointain intérieur* [1938], in *Plume, suivi de Lointain intérieur*, Paris: Gallimard, 1985.

169 Conversations with Gabrielle Palasse-Labrunie, 1996–2014, and interviews with Claude Delay-Tubiana, 1997–1998.

170 Paul Morand, *The Allure of Chanel* (1976), illustrated by Karl Lagerfeld, London: Pushkin Press, 2013, p. 200.

171 Personal archives.

172 Foreword by Patrick Mauriès in Louise de Vilmorin, *Mémoires de Coco*, p. 9.

173 'Le New Look: aux origines de l'histoire Dior,' film by Antoine Lachand produced by Lionel Quantin, France Culture, rebroadcast on 2 August 2019 (first broadcast on 16 April 2012, on the programme 'Sur les Docks').

174 Conversations with Gabrielle Palasse-Labrunie, 1996–2014.

175 Personal archives.

176 Conversations with Gabrielle Palasse-Labrunie, 1996–2014.

177 Walter Schellenberg, *Memoiren*, Cologne: Verlag für Politik und Wirtschaft, 1959, p. 9. Schellenberg's memoirs were published in English under the title *The Labyrinth: Memoirs of Walter Schellenberg, Hitler's Chief of Counterintelligence*, trans. Louis Hagen, New York: Harper, 1956.

178 Interview with Klaus Harpprecht, 2016.

179 Interviews with Reinhard Doerries in 1998–1999, then 2016.

180 Conversations with Gabrielle Palasse-Labrunie, 1996–2014.

181 Interview with Stanley Marcus, September 1999.

182 Michel Déon, *Bagages pour Vancouver* [1985], Paris: Gallimard, 1987, p. 24.

183   Colette, *Prisons et paradis* [1932], Paris: Fayard, 1986, p. 112.
184   Typed note by René de Chambrun, 'Gabrielle Chanel as I knew her, admired and supported her, 1934–1971', private archives.
185   Interviews with Robert Goossens, in his workshop in Saint-Denis, March 1997 and in May 1998.
186   Interview with Michelle Perrot, 13 February 2015; notably, along with Georges Duby, she edited *Histoire des femmes en Occident* [1991], 5 vols., Paris: Perrin, 2008.
187   *Vogue*, 15 February 1954.
188   1998 interview with Jean Mermod in Lausanne.
189   Conversations with Gabrielle Palasse-Labrunie, 1996–2014.
190   The rumours 'originated, in the opinion of Madame Charles-Roux, from the Paris ballet master who had been closely associated with Madame Chanel for years and who was to benefit from a bequest in her will, which, to his great disappointment, did not happen.' This can be read in a note from Theodor Momm following his interview with Edmonde Charles-Roux on 24 April 1974 (private archives). Also in conversations with Gabrielle Palasse-Labrunie, 1996–2014.
191   Interview with Jean Mermod in Lausanne, 1998.
192   Interviews with Claude Delay-Tubiana, 1997–1998.
193   1998 interviews with Robert Badinter in his office on the rue Guynemer, and with René de Chambrun, at his home on the place du Palais-Bourbon.
194   Interview with Gabrielle Palasse-Labrunie, Claude Delay-Tubiana, and Robert Goossens.
195   Interviews with Claude Delay-Tubiana, 1997–1998.

Archive sources

In France:

Departmental archives of Allier, Charente-Maritime,
Corrèze, Finistère, Gard, Indre-et-Loire,
Maine-et-Loire, Paris, Puy-de-Dôme, Var.

Municipal archives of Aubenas, Brive-la-Gaillarde,
Clermont-Ferrand, Courpière, Fréjus, Guéret, Issoire,
Moulins, Nîmes, Ponteils-et-Brésis, Quimper, Saintes,
Saumur, Varennes-sur-Allier, Vichy.

Compagnie de Vichy / Compagnie Fermière de
l'Établissement Thermal de Vichy (CFV).

Theosophical Society of France.

Bibliothèque Nationale de France.

Inathèque de France.

Museum of Decorative Arts.

French Institute of Fashion.

French National Archives.

French Ministry of the Interior.

French Ministry of the Armed Forces.

Service Historique de la Défense (SHD), Historical
Archive Centre, Vincennes and Cherbourg.

Archives of the Paris Police Prefecture.

Institute of the History of the Current Age (IHTP), CNRS.
Contemporary Jewish Documentation Centre (CDJC).
Private archives.

In Germany:

Bundesarchiv, Berlin.
Bundesnachrichtendienst (BND), Berlin.
Municipal archives of Hanover.

In Great Britain:

The National Archives, Kew, Richmond.
Churchill Archives Centre, Churchill College, Cambridge.
The Malcolm Muggeridge Society, Eythorne, Kent.
Brighton Municipal Archives.

In the USA:

National Archives and Records Administration (NARA),
    Military & Intelligence, College Park, Maryland.
Malcolm Muggeridge Archives, Wheaton College, Illinois.

Selected bibliography

Edmonde Charles-Roux, *Chanel: Her Life, Her World,
the Woman Behind the Legend*, London: MacLehose
Press, 2009

Claude Delay, *Chanel Solitaire*, New York: Quadrangle/
New York Times Book Company, 1974

Pierre Galante, with Philippe Orsini, *Mademoiselle Chanel*,
Washington, DC: H. Regnery Company, 1973

Arthur Gold and Robert Fizdale, *Misia: The Life
of Misia Sert*, New York: Morrow Quill, 1981

Marcel Haedrich, *Coco Chanel secrète*, Paris:
Robert Laffont, 1971

Marcel Haedrich, *Coco Chanel*, Paris: Belfond, 1987

Jean Leymarie, *Eternal Chanel*, London: Thames
& Hudson, 2010

Paul Morand, *Lewis and Irene*, New York: Boni &
Liveright, 1925

Paul Morand, *The Allure of Chanel*, edited and illustrated
by Karl Lagerfeld, London: Pushkin Press, 2013

Louise de Vilmorin, *Mémoires de Coco*, ed. Patrick Mauriès
with Martina Cardelli, Paris: Le Promeneur, 1999

Illustration captions

p. 10: Portrait of Coco Chanel at around twenty-five years old (© CHANEL – Private archives / All rights reserved).

p. 30: Coco with André Palasse as a child. This is one of the few photographs she kept (private collection).

p. 46: Coco with Boy Capel, 1910. She is wearing jodhpurs, at a time when most women wore corsets and rode sidesaddle (© CHANEL – Private archives / All rights reserved).

p. 62: Coco in Étretat, c. 1913, in one of her early jersey ensembles (© CHANEL – Private archives / All rights reserved).

p. 76: Coco in a high-backed armchair, photographed by Horst P. Horst in 1937 (© Photo by Horst P. Horst / Condé Nast / Getty Images).

p. 92: Coco wearing the emerald necklace given to her by the Duke of Westminster in the 1930s (© CHANEL – Private archives / All rights reserved).

p. 110: Coco as the figurehead for Chanel N°5, photographed in 1937 in her suite at the Ritz by François Kollar for *Harper's Bazaar* (© Ministère de la Culture – Médiathèque du Patrimoine, Dist. RMN-Grand Palais / François Kollar).

p. 134: Coco photographed by Boris Lipnitzki in 1937, with one of her many Coromandel screens (© Boris Lipnitzki / Roger Viollet).

p. 148: Coco on her beige couch, reading *L'Orient musulman*: she often said 'My finest journeys were made on this couch.' This 1938 photograph by Jean Moral shows her wearing her 'little yellow ring', as always (Jean Moral, 1938 © Brigitte Moral SAIF Paris).

p. 160 : Coco photographed by Roger Schall in 1937 in her studio at 31 rue Cambon (photo Roger Schall © Schall Collection).

p. 176 : Coco photographed by Mike de Dulmen in 1957 in her apartment at 31 rue Cambon. Her everyday surroundings include a statuette of a lion and countless leather-bound books (photo Mike de Dulmen © All rights reserved).

p. 195: Coco photographed by Horst P. Horst in 1937. White was always the colour of mourning to her (© Horst P. Horst / Condé Nast / Getty Images).

p. 214: André Palasse and his daughter Tiny in Switzerland after the war, outside the chalet Harmonie, which Coco had rented (private collection).

Acknowledgments

Thanks to Tiny, a.k.a. Gabrielle Palasse-Labrunie. Without our friendship, without our conversations from 1996 to 2014, this book simply would not exist. As the daughter of André Palasse and the granddaughter or great-niece of Coco Chanel, she was close and intimate with her for more than forty years.

Thanks to Guillaume Labrunie, son of Tiny, for his long-lasting friendship and support; thanks to Véronique and Marine.

Thanks to Claude Delay-Tubiana, Carole Bouquet, Jacques Polge, Robert Badinter, René de Chambrun, Robert Goossens, Jean Mermod, Quitterie Tempé, Annie Girardot, Delphine de Bonneval.

Thanks to Michelle Perrot, Florence Müller, Emmanuelle Montet, Dominique Veillon, Sophie Kurkdjian, Jean Lebrun, Dominique Marny, Prince Michel Romanoff, Vanina de Planta.

Thanks to Colette and Paul Valaude and Father Henri Fouques in Courpière; Dominique Legrand, Marie-Noëlle Piquet and Françoise de Vergnette in Moulins; Irmgard Muller in Lausanne; Stanley Marcus in Dallas, Priya Giri and Killian Jordan of *Life* and Nancy Harris of *The New York Times* in New York.

Thank you to the entire Patrimoine de Chanel team, especially Hélène Fulgence, Odile Prémel, Marika Genty, Patrick Doucet, Laura Draghici-Foulon; and, above all, to Cécile Goddet-Dirles.

Thank you Mario Pasa for his invaluable help.

Finally, on the war period:

Thank you to Sir Stuart Hampshire and Paul Elston in Britain; Niels Gordes and Morris Izlar in the USA; Reinhard R. Doerries in Germany; Klaus Harpprecht, Henry Rousso, Patricia Gillet, Lucile Chartain, Monique Leblois-Péchon, Frédéric Quéguineur, Pascal Raimbault, Jean-Yves Lorant, Sarah Halperin; and for the Malcolm Muggeridge information: Sally Muggeridge, David Malone, Jean-Paul Avice and David Simon.

Thank you to all those who helped me at the Ministry of the Interior and the Ministry of the Armed Forces. Thank you to all those who, whether in French intelligence or wishing to remain anonymous, facilitated my research in France and Germany.